PRAISE FOR *LEARN TO FLY*

"In *Learn to Fly*, Dr. Okolo offers an inspiring and relatable account of her remarkable journey as a black female aerospace engineer. Through engaging storytelling and actionable insights, she empowers readers, particularly those from underrepresented backgrounds to overcome obstacles and pursue their goals in the complex world of STEM.

This book is a beacon of hope, reminding us of the power of persistence and the transformative impact of unwavering determination, which can be applied to all works of life."

- Kareen Okaka
  Author of *Being Brave*

"If a journey of a thousand miles begins with a single step, *Learn To Fly* starts with and reiterates a belief, a conviction that one's horizons are absolutely unlimited as Dr. Okolo's skies. On the wings of determination, our dreams will soar."

- Dr. Erian Armanios
President, American Society for Composites
Fellow, American Institute of Aeronautics & Astronautics
Chair, Mechanical & Aerospace Engineering Department at the University of Texas at Arlington.

"Dr. Okolo's vivid and elegant storytelling takes readers on an exhilarating journey through the life of a minority aerospace engineering student. A captivating memoir, *Learn to Fly* is a must-read for anyone interested in science, technology, engineering, and mathematics – or pursuing their dreams against all odds."

- Dr. Kola Ogunsina
  Operations Data Scientist, Jetblue Airways

"Dr. Wendy Okolo's book, *Learn to Fly* is an engaging and insightful look into her journey to being an aerospace engineer as she navigates through family, society, and self. She shares knowledge in a warm, accessible storytelling style balanced with relevant and current examples from the aerospace and academic cultures that resonate and are applicable for everyone. I will certainly add *Learn to Fly* nuggets as a key resource in my continuing work as a coach with early career folks and others, and most importantly, with my family's own next generation."

- Karen C. Bradford
NASA Ames Research Center
Director, Strategic Partnerships (Retired)
Executive Coach

"*Learn to Fly* feels like a conversation with your favorite older sister. Author Dr. Wendy Okolo has a way of weaving life advice into comical anecdotes that bring her personal story to life. Whether interested in a STEM field or not, the message "everything is for everyone" rings throughout with practical applications to any field. This story will spark a reader's ambition and equip them with the tools to find their own path to success."

- Alexandra "Allie" Jannetta
Project Manager, MIT Horizons

"*Learn to Fly* leaves no stone unturned when it comes to navigating the ins and outs of what it takes to land a successful career. It is a page-turner filled with wit, positive affirmations, and relatable life events. Dr. Wendy A. Okolo carefully details her journey through the highs, lows, struggles, and triumphs, all of which drive home the importance of hard work, grit, and determination. Each chapter leaves the reader equipped with gems and tools that can be leveraged and applied to any line of study. *Learn to Fly*: A Remarkable Must-Read Manual for All."

- Imharia Obiagba
Contract Manager, Johnson & Johnson

LEARN TO FLY

On Becoming a Rocket Scientist

Wendy A. Okolo, Ph.D.
Aerospace Research Engineer

E4E PRESS LTD. CO.

Cover design by Brand'ee Milton
Cover photograph by Afolabi Mosuro
Background cover photograph by Wendy A. Okolo

Printed in the United States of America
First Edition: June 2023

Published by E4E Press Ltd. Co. The publisher is not responsible for websites (or content) that are not owned by the publisher. To contact Dr. Wendy A. Okolo for speaking events, please visit www.wendyokolo.com/contact.

ISBN: 979-8-9883068-0-1

Alex P. N. Okolo:
You remind me to get the tough out when the going
gets tough.
I carry you with me, now and forever, Daddy.

This book is designed to provide information for readers in the pursuit of scholastic success. It offers helpful tips and education, but it is not projected to be a full-service solution in the quest for knowledge. Information in this book is general in nature and offered with no guarantees on the part of the author or E4E Press Ltd. Co. Neither the author nor E4E Press Ltd. Co. shall be held liable or responsible for any loss or damage allegedly arising from any suggestion or information contained in this book. Unless explicitly noted, the names and identifying details of people associated with events described in this book have been changed.

FOREWORD

By Donald G. James

"What an elder sees sitting, a young person cannot see,
even if they climb a tree."
African Proverb

Picture an aerospace engineer. What image comes to mind? Chances are they don't look like or have a name like Wendy Okolo: female; black; Nigerian-born; Igbo. At 16, Okolo moved to Texas to begin her university education, and ten years later, at the age of 26, she received her PhD in Aerospace Engineering – the first black woman to do so at the University of Texas, Arlington. Later, she won the Black Engineer of the Year Award for being "the most promising engineer in the United States government." Read that last line again. Carefully.

How did she do it? How did she overcome the obstacles that surely stood in her way? Dr. Okolo's path was not paved with gold bricks melded with privileged grout, nor is it a rags-to-riches story. It's a story of focus, determination, perseverance, high standards, self-awareness, and impeccable manners (my favorite, I must confess). And if you read carefully, you'll realize Dr. Okolo had some good fortune. She was lucky to be born to parents who had high expectations for her and her siblings and who loved them unconditionally.

You would be forgiven if, at first glance, you assume this book is about learning how to pilot an aircraft. However, there is no "how" in the title, nor is there any mention of "aircraft", "spacecraft," or any mechanical aerial vehicle for that matter. This clever title hints at something deeper. The reader who understands this wisdom will be served well.

If you are a student reading this, congratulations. Before you is a useful and practical guide to "flying", whether it IS an aircraft or spacecraft, or any career you choose. Metaphorically, "flying" implies getting off the ground, overcoming the laws of gravity, and finding your path and destination. There was a time when the idea of humans defying gravity and "flying" was deemed ludicrous. What seems ludicrous to you now that you need to transcend? Read this book and be inspired to discover your way past ludicrousness.

If you are the parent or guardian of a promising young engineer or scientist, then take note. Your role is critical to your charge's success. Set high standards, provide tools, and love them. It also helps to walk the talk. That is your responsibility. And remember, there is no "how" in *Learn To Fly*. The student creates the how.

Dr. Okolo's candor in *Learn to Fly* is refreshing. She shares her vulnerabilities and how she managed delicate situations. She takes responsibility for her actions and outcomes. She is no victim, even when she had a right to be. Remember in math class where just writing the right answer was insufficient to demonstrate competency? You were required to "show your work." In *Learn To Fly*, Dr. Okolo is not afraid to show her work while also teaching a little math and science. It's a fun read and will make you say, "That's cool; I didn't know that."

I had the pleasure of working at NASA Ames Research Center in Northern California, where Dr. Okolo works. It seemed she was always everywhere and in demand. Always participating, learning, and giving. She carries her responsibilities with elegance and grace and knows that who she is means something to people.

I challenge the reader to get to know Dr. Wendy A. Okolo and see what she and *Learn To Fly* mean to you. It may well be the key to getting past what, for you now, seems ludicrous.

Donald G. James
NASA Associate Administrator for Education (Retired)
Pleasanton, CA
2023

There are many ways to the stars.
May this book help you find your way.

-- **Wendy**

CONTENTS

Motivation

How did she do that at 26? A Ph.D.? Can she respond and let all of us know? How did she fund the degrees? Come on NASA tell us more! Her full story can and will inspire all students!

This is a real comment under a LinkedIn post by NASA. The NASA. The National Aeronautics and Space Administration: the same one that landed people on the moon and is responsible for the creation of remarkable technology from memory foam to firefighting equipment, to freeze-dried food and cochlear implants.

In 2019, NASA nominated me for the Black Engineer of the Year Award (BEYA) for Most Promising Engineer in the United States (U.S.) government. It was a true honor to be recognized by my NASA peers and black leaders at the forefront of engineering and technology in the U.S. I won the award and attended the fancy black-tie gala and award ceremony at the annual BEYA conference in Washington, DC.

After the beautiful ceremony, I returned home to Mountain View, in the center of Silicon

Valley, California and shared a BEYA press release about my award on my social media pages. With only a few hundred followers on all my social media pages combined, I didn't expect much of it. However, my one tweet led to a retweet and news of the award and press release went viral.

NASA - National Aeronautics and Space Administration
6,332,396 followers
3yr · 🌐

Wendy Okolo has wanted to be an engineer for as long as she could remember. She earned her Ph.D. in aerospace engineering at age 26 and now works as an aerospace research engineer at NASA. In 2019 she wa ... see more

BLACK HISTORY MONTH

Wendy A. Okolo, Ph.D.
Aerospace Research Engineer

I woke up the following day to thousands of mentions on Twitter, Instagram, and LinkedIn. My email and call logs were not spared either. I couldn't understand why. *What was it about the award?* It was a career highlight for me, but I didn't think other people would care till I did a little more digging.

The press release contained a brief biography of me with one tiny but important detail:

At 26, Dr. Wendy Okolo became the first woman to earn a Ph.D. in aerospace engineering from the University of Texas at Arlington.

People were more interested in *that* story. *How does a young Nigerian girl get a Ph.D. in aerospace engineering at 26? Can my daughter get one too? How about just a bachelor's degree in aerospace engineering? Can I work as an aerospace engineer with a mechanical engineering degree?* Things I had just done—getting a bachelor's degree and getting a Ph.D. afterwards—were apparently trailblazing. *Really?* The BEYA award and working at NASA, although interesting enough, didn't pique as much curiosity as the aerospace engineering degree . . . and so, the requests came flooding in.

I received and honored speaking requests from within and outside the continental U.S. From companies and organizations such as Jeff Bezos' Blue Origin, to the Association of Professional Engineers and Geoscientists of Alberta, Canada. I spoke to Corona schools in Lagos, Nigeria and Ashesi university in Berekuso, Ghana. I gave keynotes at conferences of the Girls Scouts to inspire young women in science, technology, engineering, and mathematics (STEM) and at TechPlus, Africa's largest Technology Conference and Exposition. I even returned to my university and gave the keynote speech at the 2019 convocation ceremony.

In addition to speaking about fun aerospace work and demystifying the aerospace engineering field, there was an underlying theme of these requests: How? The same questions kept arising from students in middle school, high school, and university to parents requesting mentoring for their children, and even early career professionals navigating employment opportunities and promotions. After speaking about the mechanics of guided spacecraft entry and descent into Mars at the 2019 Silicon Valley Comic Con, I got off the stage and received the same question from a young woman:

"I want to be an aerospace engineer too. Do you have any advice for me?"

I realized three surprising things. The first was that people found my story inspirational, but more importantly, valuable, as demonstrated by the written and verbal testimonials I received after each talk. Each speaking engagement required me to reflect on the key turning points that led me to success and failure as I contemplated my academic and professional trajectory. It's one thing to tell people to "work hard and persevere" but what exactly does that translate to in terms of tangible actionable advice? Whenever I spoke to people wanting to know the "how," I made sure to include tractable how-to information.

The second surprising thing I realized was that the percentage of minorities and underrepresented people in STEM is still bleak. I should have known this because my aerospace engineering classes routinely only had two or three females and twenty to thirty males. In fact, I was the only black girl in my aerospace engineering classes. However, I didn't think much of it. I just went through the rigors of school like everybody else.

It's interesting because in the mid-twentieth century, it was commonplace to see black people in science, technology, engineering, and mathematics. Aerospace-related fields were no exception as demonstrated by Margot Lee Shetterly through the story depicted in the 2016 film *Hidden Figures*: How did a team of female African-American mathematicians play a vital role at NASA during the early years of the U.S. space program? In the book by the same name, Shetterly painted a picture of how normal it was for black residents in Newport News, Virginia, to work as mathematicians at the NASA Langley Research Center in Virginia. Unfortunately, the numbers dwindled over time, and black female aerospace engineers and mathematicians became the exception, rather than the rule.

Although the numbers remain paltry, many individuals and organizations are working to change the narrative of underrepresentation in STEM. From Virgin Atlantic and Barbie, who introduced pilot and engineer barbie dolls through the Dream Gap Project, to Zonta International, who has commemorated the memory of the avant-garde Amelia Earhart through a Ph.D. fellowship for women in aerospace related fields to the U.S. Department of State through the TechWomen program for women in STEM living in Africa, Central and South Asia and the Middle East. A lot is happening but not enough is changing.

This leads me to my third realization: As additional international press features precipitated new requests—from Mauritius to Malawi and from the United Kingdom to Brazil—I realized that I needed to streamline my message. I simply could not answer everyone's questions from a podium or a stage. I also couldn't keep up with the mentoring requests. I had to consider more widespread dissemination for the same repeated questions, so I could simply point people to a platform with the content they needed. I also needed to do my part on a larger scale to positively influence the outlook of underrepresentation in STEM fields.

These realizations form the rationale for the creation of this book, *Learn To Fly*. *Learn to Fly* documents the strategic steps I took to become an aerospace engineer, the fortuitous ones, the mistakes I made, and the ones I saw others make. As expected, there are losses with the wins, and I share those too.

Although this book recounts my undergraduate academic experiences, it is a guide to facilitate successful learning in a formal academic environment, independent of your academic standing, level, or field. Success runs the gamut from how to ace a class to how to get a mentor in your field to how to make the most of your job or internship. Even now that I'm older and established in my aerospace engineering career, I still rely on the lessons I learned as a 16-year-old university student.

A Ph.D. in aerospace engineering at 26?
My name is Wendy and I'll tell you how.

Introduction

In 2008, I sat in the office of one of my undergraduate aerospace engineering (AE) professors. I was exactly a year and a half away from graduating, so things were getting *real*. I was now learning how to characterize the aerodynamics of slow-moving fluids and how to calculate the parameters for spacecraft orbiting the moon, earth, and other celestial bodies. *What a time to be alive!*

Well, it would have been a time to be alive if I wasn't in my professor's office to discuss my grades. I had just gotten some disappointing test scores back in one of my classes and I was displeased. So was my professor. He asked, "What's happening? I thought you would be the Trevor of this class." I paused. Although I was unhappy at my performance, I was slightly flattered that my reputation preceded me, to the point where I was likened to a brilliant male student who was my senior. We all knew Trevor: He was the smart white guy and the poster child for aerospace engineering student perfection.

As my mind drifted, I briefly contemplated whether discussions about student performance were standard practice in the MAE professors' break room. However, I doubted that a busy tenure-track professor would know or care about how intelligent a second or third-year student was. Another theory that came to mind was that professors looked up students' grades and academic histories before the first day of class, so they'd know the percentages of hoodlums and Einsteins they would have to deal with. *That had to be it!* Alas, it was not. The U.S. Family and Educational Rights and Privacy Act (FERPA) protects the privacy of students' prior records unless there is a legitimate educational need for a professor to know. *Was there a legitimate need for him to know? If so, what was it?*

I dragged my wandering mind back to the matter at hand. Frankly, my reputation served me no purpose if I wasn't getting an A in the class.

He repeated, "I am disappointed. What is wrong and why aren't you getting it?"

I leaned back into the chair and shrugged my shoulders. "Honestly, I'm turned off in your class. You go through the material quickly. There's barely any time for questions because you have a lot to cover."

Crossing my arms, I continued my diatribe, "The one time we had a dedicated problem-solving session in class, your teaching assistant ran it. All she did was copy problems and solutions on the board." He listened intently as I carried on, "It's not a great learning experience. It's just not working!"

I was more fearless at the time with significantly fewer inhibitions. I miss the boldness of that feisty student, but I realize I could have been more graceful with my response. It wasn't all his fault, and here's why.

My professor taught one of the more complex yet fascinating classes of my baccalaureate career, at the juncture where the previously similar aerospace engineering and mechanical engineering curriculum began to diverge. Our curriculum was extensive and needed to fit within a four-year track. It was made even more challenging with certain prerequisite classes offered only once a year.

In addition, good *ol'* Texas required all undergraduate students to complete a forty-two-semester credit hour core curriculum of non-engineering courses before receiving a bachelor's degree; two American history classes, two political science classes, two communications courses, two English classes... and the list goes on. In fact, I once overheard an engineering professor lamenting over how Texas college engineering programs had to fit all these basic courses into the curriculum, leaving little room for the real engineering courses.

This was my professor's dilemma. In fact, there was a prerequisite for his class that was removed before my time. Our poor professor had to combine material from the prerequisite course into the now ostensibly tough course and teach at a pace that would impress the maddest of scientists: Write swiftly on the board, erase with alacrity, and talk like he was in competition with Twista for the Guinness World Record for fastest rapper.

I reiterated, "It's just not working. Even the textbook doesn't help. The material you cover in class is not in the textbook."

Unfazed by my grumbling, my professor kindly recommended two additional textbooks for me. I wrote down the textbook titles, but I hesitated a little because (A) I didn't believe another textbook would solve the problem and (B) I was a struggling college student on financial aid and scholarships, without the money or desire to buy additional textbooks. I mean buying the required textbooks for my classes was one thing, but buying two additional textbooks for one class was just uncalled for. *I mean who does that?*

So, I went online and reviewed the first book. This book had the content for the prerequisite class, which I didn't even know was a prerequisite. It was great, easy to follow, and quite frankly, beautiful to read. Was I going to buy it? Nope! Instead, I checked my school's library, the library of my best friend's school in Houston, TX, and the library of my sister's medical school in Galveston, Texas. I was more familiar with the library websites of friends and family than said friends and family were. I lucked out with one of them and got an older edition of the book, which I incorporated into my study material, changing my trajectory in that class.

At the end of the semester, two people got an A in the class—only two, out of two dozen students. I was one of them. I kept my 4.0 GPA and lived to battle another semester.

I completed my undergraduate degree and went even further for graduate studies, becoming the first black woman to obtain a Ph.D. in aerospace engineering at the University of Texas at Arlington. Now I am an aerospace research engineer at NASA, and often I get the question of *how* from parents and students alike, particularly those from underrepresented groups like me. *How did you do it?* It's an ingenuous question but it requires a nuanced answer, something beyond the standard "work hard, listen, and believe" response.

My "how" is my story. It is unique to me and in this book, I will use my story as a guide to teach you how to learn hard things. You can also consider my story a fun introduction to aerospace engineering.

Your story, of course, will be unique to you. My hope is that the lessons I experienced and reflected on will inspire you too to achieve your goals. I don't have all the answers, but I do have some stories from my baccalaureate journey that are prescriptive of problems we all face when we want to learn something complex. These stories remind even me, who experienced them, what persistence and diligence look like. There will always be challenges but my hope is that my challenges, with both good and disappointing outcomes, help you handle and persevere through yours.

I pray that sharing my journey helps someone who is stuck or who may feel like science, technology, engineering, or mathematics (STEM) is just too hard. Or maybe my stories just make you laugh and inspire you to build a spaceship that takes you to Mars (please make room for me if you do). Whatever it is, I pray that before you quit, you remember that there are many ways to the stars. May this book and my story help you find your way.

Before College

Don't Listen To The Critics

When I was a child, I wanted two things: to be an engineer and to be left alone. My desire to be left alone prompted me to even skip recess and breaktime at school. I didn't want a speck of dirt on my perfectly pleated cyan Catholic school uniform, or God forbid, to be pushed by another child and risk bruising my knee. I loved my talking V-tech Whiz Kid learning tablet, and that wonder of technology, too, was sheltered by me. Only on rare occasions would I share it with a few careful friends. They had to come over to my house and sit quietly to use it: No vigorous button pushing, throwing, or fighting over it was allowed. Sometimes, I even wanted to be left alone by my older sisters, Phyllis and Jennifer, who were content to let me take over the big television in the living room and watch Tom and Jerry and Cinderella on repeat. I could recite the latter cartoon word for word.

While this childhood mannerism offered ample room for me to explore, grow, and ultimately envision my future, now as an adult, I've learned that being left alone is not conducive to being an engineer. Engineers regularly work as members of a team, and they must work well with others. But even as a child, a female Nigerian child, people found it interesting that I wanted to be an engineer. So, they didn't quite leave me alone. I was a source of both fascination and cynicism to adults.

My parents put engineering in my head before I could even spell the word. I was the third child of Nigerian parents, and like many of their peers in the early 90s, they decided their children's careers. The pickings were slim. You could be a doctor, lawyer, engineer, perhaps an accountant, or you could move out of the house. I had two older sisters, and they were already assigned the paths of doctor and lawyer, so when I came along, I would be the engineer and that was that.

Having that decision made for you as a child can be a gift or a curse. It is a curse if you are expected to be a medical doctor and have no interest in the sciences, for example. This scenario can lead to feelings of failure and resentment: *Hello to therapy at twenty-nine!* For me, it was a gift because I happened to like math and the sciences, and I was pretty good at anything theoretical. Also, I didn't have to figure it out or scramble to respond whenever I got asked what I wanted to be when I grew up. Beaming with confidence, I would proudly respond, "An engineer!"

Well, that response didn't work out for me one day in elementary school in Lagos, Nigeria. My third-grade teacher Ms. Obi asked us what we were going to be when we grew up. Table by table, seat by seat, we stood up and declared our grown-up plans to the class. When it got to me, I stood tall and said, "I want to be an engineer!" First, there was a brief silence as it dawned on Ms. Obi what I had just said. The students were also quiet as most pupils learn from an early age not to speak out of turn in school.

What I thought was no big deal was apparently a very big deal. It was clear that no girl had ever said, out loud in Ms. Obi's classroom, that she wanted to be an engineer. After a long, painful silence (we knew to let the teacher lead), Ms. Obi said, "You want to be an engineer? You want to fix ceiling fans for a living?" She jabbed a finger to the wobbly fan circling above us. There was another brief silence, and then Ms. Obi's sharp cackle erupted like an alarm, echoing in the room, followed by a wave of nervous giggles from the rest of my peers.

That ordeal was surely the most embarrassing experience of my six-year-old life.

When I got home from school that day, I recounted the experience to my mother. I told her in no uncertain terms that I no longer wanted to be an engineer. "Mommy, my teacher said I'll be fixing ceiling fans."

Mama was livid! She had a few choice words for the teacher but more importantly, a few inspiring words for me. She told me about all the cool things engineers did like inventing, designing, and maintaining all kinds of structures and machines. From cars and skyscrapers to planes and prosthetic arms.

My mother was not an engineer, but she was able to reinforce and encourage me not to change my mind. By doing so, she gave me my first pair of wings and showed me I could fly. I put the humiliating incident behind me and ignored my teacher, who honestly just didn't know better. I committed myself to excelling at everything but particularly my science, mathematics, and advanced mathematics courses, and I still said, "I want to be an engineer," whenever I was asked.

~~~~~~~~~~~~~~~~~~~~~~~~~~~~~~~~

LEARN TO FLY NUGGET: NO ONE IS EXEMPT FROM ADVERSITY. NOT A SIX-

YEAR-OLD CHILD AND DEFINITELY
NOT YOU. THAT'S OK. LIFE GOES ON.

~~~~~~~~~~~~~~~~~~~~~~~~~~~~~~~~~~~~~

When I got into Queen's College, Yaba, a competitive all-girls secondary school[1] in Lagos, I learned that our junior secondary science class would be split into physics, chemistry, and biology. Each science class period, we focused on only one of the three science disciplines. I enjoyed biology and learning about plants and animals. When we learned about osmosis and diffusion, I already knew what they were. My big sister had taught me about diffusion when I was in elementary school. She said, "Wendy, when you fart and I can smell it from all the way over here, it's because the atoms and molecules of your fart move from a region of high concentration around you, to a region of low concentration around me, through a process called diffusion." I didn't appreciate my flatulence being used as a reference for something I didn't even ask to learn so I tartly responded, "No, it only happens

---

[1] Secondary school refers to schooling after elementary school and before a university education in the United Kingdom and most countries in Africa. Imagine combining middle school and high school into one comprehensive learning institution for children aged 10/11 years to 16/17 years old.

when you fart!" We both laughed but that explanation stuck with me.

Although I liked biology, biology didn't like me too much. One time, we were asked to draw and label a fish, showing its eyes, mouth, gill, and fins. I drew the perfect fish with the perfect oval shape. I may have even used a plastic protractor for the outline. My teacher expeditiously noted on my graded drawing that my fish looked lifeless. I didn't understand why that was a problem. My perfectly structured fish clearly depicted the mouth, eyes, gill, and fins. *What more could she want?* I mean this wasn't an arts class and I wasn't Salvatore Dali.

Alas, now I know that we all have a creative right-brain and an analytical left-brain. If your creative side dominates, you're better at drawing, décor, and design. If your analytical left-brain dominates, then logic, reason, and numbers are your forte. My biology fish saga was my first indicator that my analytical left-brained side dominated my creative right-brained side. I consistently got low As and high Bs in biology, as opposed to the high As I received in physics and chemistry, which were more theoretical.

Build a Resume and Relationships

In Nigeria, students are required to declare one of three major courses of study during our senior secondary school, based on their junior secondary final exam scores: arts, commercial, or science. This declaration is dependent on what students want to study in university.

Students that would study law and similar courses of study are arts students and are required to take history and government classes, in addition to the core secondary school curriculum with basic mathematics and English. Commercial students take business and accounting courses to become accountants and businesspeople. Science students comprise of anyone who wants to pursue a Science, Technology, Engineering, or Mathematics (STEM) degree in university. As a future engineer, I declared that would be a science student.

There were a few of us girls that wanted to be engineers and had possibly overcome the Ms. Obis in our lives. We bonded over our love for the sciences and routinely talked about our future engineering plans. "Where would we go to university? Who would move to the UK or the U.S.? What kind of engineering would we do?"

We walked to our physics building together and carried out measurements while carefully gazing directly above the tick marks on the ruler or scale. Heaven forbid we acceded to the pervasive error due to parallax that occurs when you skew your measurements by reading the tick marks at an angle. We used Bunsen burners and tried not to set our chemistry lab ablaze when conducting chemistry experiments that generated all sorts of horrible smelling gases. We carried our French curves, drafting boards, and rulers to our remote and uncompleted technical drawing building, where we created isometric drawings with perfect thirty-, sixty-, and ninety-degree angles. In geography, we studied varying climates, seismic activity, latitudes, and longitudes of different parts of the Earth. Finally, in our further mathematics class, we learned that if y depends on x, then we can determine (by hand) how quickly y changes as x is changed. We learned that the change is called a *derivative* and it can be represented by something called dy/dx. How fascinating!

Further mathematics was one of my favorite classes, and I began to find ordinary mathematics boring. In further mathematics, all we needed was a pen and some paper. Why use a calculator in mathematics to determine the derivative for a function of y dependent on x when I could simply use my trusty Bic pen and a sheet of paper in further mathematics? The latter was more fun and that's where the action was.

At 15, I graduated from Queen's College. I didn't have much of a resume nor did I consider writing one. I hadn't been involved in any extracurricular activities or clubs at school, though some of my peers were. My non-scholastic involvement centered around the Catholic church a short walk from home, even when there was no mass. I was there almost every day after school, and it was a social hangout spot for me. I had been in the children's choir and eventually in the adult choir. I was a member of the church dance team and would routinely perform at major church events. I also tried my hand at the drama but didn't spend too much time there. In retrospect, these were all great activities to list on the resume of a high-school graduate, but I didn't consider them worthy at the time.

~~~~~~~~~~~~~~~~~~~~~~~~~~~~~~~

LEARN TO FLY NUGGET: IT'S NEVER TOO EARLY TO BUILD YOUR RESUME. CONSIDER ALL YOU DO IN AND

OUTSIDE SCHOOL. PERHAPS YOU TUTOR MIDDLE SCHOOLERS AS A HIGH SCHOOLER. HAVE A RESUME YOU CAN BUILD ON.

~~~~~~~~~~~~~~~~~~~~~~~~~~~~~~~~

Here is a sample resume template for a typical high school student interested in STEM:

SAMPLE RESUME FOR HIGH SCHOOL/SECONDARY SCHOOL STUDENT

Your Name (First and Last name)
Your Email Address (Ideally firstname_lastname@gmail.com, no babyGirl4Lyf@yahoo.com, I beg you!)
Address or at least City and State
Working Phone Number

EDUCATION
Queen's College Yaba (QCY) Secondary School, Lagos Nigeria
Your classification/level (Senior, etc.)
Relevant Coursework: Advanced Mathematics, Technical Drawing, Organic Chemistry, *etc.*
Honors: National Dean's List, National Society of Collegiate Scholars, *etc.*
Clubs: Chess club, drama club, *etc.*

COMPUTER SKILLS
Proficient in MS Office – Word, Excel, and PowerPoint
Basic Knowledge of Adobe Photoshop

WORK EXPERIENCES

Incept Company, Social Media Handler

- Managed the online presence for the Incept Security Company.
- Created a following of 1500 people on Instagram, 2000 on TikTok, and 670 on LinkedIn.

EXTRACURRICULAR ACTIVITIES

Class Captain (2020 – 2021)

- Served as the liaison between the QCY class of 2023 and the school's academic and administrative staff.
- Initiated the development of an inexpensive yearbook for the graduating class of 2023, reducing costs by 20% in comparison to prior years.

Soccer Club (2020 – 2022)

- Goalkeeper for the teenage girls' soccer club at 1004 Housing Estate, Victoria Island Lagos.
- Organized tryouts every quarter to evaluate the skillsets of new recruits and team members.

AWARDS

- Nominated for the Under 18 Social Media handler of the Year Award for students in all secondary schools in the nation.
- Winner of the Thesaurus Competition for the most eloquent student in the school.

Tip: Microsoft Word has many resume templates that you can use, just plug in your information.

What I considered important upon graduating from Queen's College was obtaining a collection of recommendation letters.

Recommendation letters are used to apply for scholarships, entrance into university, or other programs. They can be somewhat generic so that you can use them for more than one purpose.

Before I said my final goodbyes, I asked for recommendation letters from my teachers, under whose tutelage I had spent the last six years. I didn't know exactly what I would need these letters for but someone somewhere (thank you to whoever that was) told me I should obtain reference letters after graduating from high school, letters that could speak about who I was in whatever capacity they knew me. Perhaps I'd need them for university admission packages and scholarship applications, or maybe I would need them for job applications. I didn't know.

All I knew was that I was leaving secondary school in the most populous city in West Africa and moving almost 7000 miles away to Dallas, Texas in the continental United States. Thus, I couldn't exactly ask resource-limited teachers, community, and even church leaders, to write email or snail mail letters of recommendation whenever I needed.

Because I didn't know if I would need these letters for potential job, university, or scholarship applications, the recommenders did not and could not specify that they were in support of a specific application. They could only state that the recommendation letters were for "Wendy Okolo" and should speak to my character, work ethic, willingness to learn, team player skills, and the like. These letters were written on general all-purpose recommendation letter sheets that looked like this:

Recommender's Full Name
Organization/Institution/Affiliation
Mailing or Physical Address
Email Address and/or Phone Number
insert letterhead if possible

Recommendation/Reference Letter for Wendy Okolo

To whom it may concern,

comments

_____

_____

_____

_____

_____

_____

Sincerely,

Recommender's Full Name

Signature

I made copies of the different letters of recommendation I received and put them away safely. These reference letters would later prove extremely valuable to me.

So, there is another tip for success before you ever set your feet on a university campus: Develop relationships with teachers and respected leaders and ask for support letters before you leave. You may not need the recommendation letters beforehand if you won't be moving to different country to start university. However, you must develop a relationship that enables you to ask a teacher or community leader to dedicate their time to writing you a strong reference letter.

Even if you do not develop these relationships, you should exhibit certain behaviors that will make referees amenable to endorsing you via a reference letter. I will provide suggestions for developing these relationships and exhibiting the right behaviors in university. These suggestions are applicable to high schoolers and others at varying levels of education. I also want to refrain from recounting my secondary school days, for brevity.

~~~~~~~~~~~~~~~~~~~~~~~~~~~~~~~~~~

LEARN TO FLY NUGGET: DEVELOP RELATIONSHIPS WITH YOUR HIGH

SCHOOL TEACHERS AND COMMUNITY
LEADERS THAT WILL ENABLE YOU TO
ASK FOR RECOMMENDATION LETTERS
WHEN YOU NEED THEM. SECURE
THOSE LETTERS BEFORE YOU LEAVE
HIGH SCHOOL, ESPECIALLY IF YOU'RE
MOVING AWAY.

~~~~~~~~~~~~~~~~~~~~~~~~~~~~~~~~~

Take the Tests Seriously

My older sisters, who let me take over the big
T.V. in the living room, were now in the U.S.—one
in medical school and the other in university. The
plan was always for me to reunite with them and my
father, God rest his soul, in the U.S. after my
secondary education. My family is both Nigerian and
American and my parents, like most Nigerian
parents at the time, wanted their children to have
their initial education and formative years in Nigeria.
After we went to primary and secondary school in
Nigeria, we were considered ready and responsible
enough to move to America for university.

My sisters told me I needed the standardized
U.S. college readiness test, the Scholastic Assessment
Test or SAT. I could take it in Nigeria, or I could

wait to take it in Dallas. After I graduated, I wasn't doing much but living my best teenage life in Lagos, hanging out with friends, and partaking in mindless gossip, learning how to drive a stick-shift using a beat-up Volkswagen with no side mirrors on the crazy Lagos streets, and keeping up with the latest hip-hop, alternative, and West African music, from Ghanaian Hiplife to Nigerian Afrobeats. It was a unanimous decision by my family that I would minimize my idleness by preparing for and taking the SAT in Lagos.

Most children in Lagos had extra tutoring for everything from classes in school to external exams like the SAT. My mother was exceptionally fond of extra tutoring for me, because her dear friend, Dr. Ify, once told her that young achievers inevitably wouldn't keep up with the rigors of the academic environment as they got older. "My sister's friend's daughter's classmate was just like Wendy, very young and intelligent. But as she got older, she just couldn't compete with her peers In school. It happens all the time," she recounted.

Dr. Ify conjectured that my older and more mature classmates would supersede me in school, leaving me far behind. I was two years younger than some of my peers because I started nursery school (kindergarten) a year early and got a double promotion in elementary school. By her theory, I would ultimately regress to peers my age, who were two years behind me in class.

Whether the theory was valid or not made no difference to my mother. She would take no chances and did everything to ensure I maintained my straight A status. Preparing for the SAT was no exception to extra tutoring. Mama promptly enrolled me in SAT prep courses at Verbum, a preparatory school for major exams and certifications, located a ten-minute walk from her office in Lagos Island, Lagos.

Alas, the SAT is now being deemed unfair to minority students lacking access to expensive test preparation classes[2]. In addition to the inequitable perception of the SAT, there is a rising sentiment that the test is not a qualitative determinant of a student's aptitude or potential to succeed in university. Thus, it is likely that some universities will make the SAT optional for admission. However, I wouldn't be so quick to disregard the SAT or not prepare for it. Even though universities may not require it for admission, scholarships and admissions into special university programs such as an honors program or honors college[3] may require scores from

---

[2] https://www.nytimes.com/2022/02/03/learning/is-taking-the-sat-a-necessary-step-in-preparing-for-post-high-school-life.html

[3] An honors program is a program within a university that offers enriching and more complex scholastic and extracurricular activities

either the SAT or its counterpart, the American College Test (ACT), which tests your understanding of your high school curriculum.

~~~~~~~~~~~~~~~~~~~~~~~~~~~~~~~~

LEARN TO FLY NUGGET: JUST BECAUSE IT'S NOT REQUIRED DOESN'T MEAN IT'S NOT USEFUL.

~~~~~~~~~~~~~~~~~~~~~~~~~~~~~~~

After preparing for the SAT by attending classes multiple days a week and taking several mock SAT exams, I finally took the exam and did well. I packed my printed SAT results, twelve reference letters, a few personal items including some math and science books (especially my trusted and worn but popular Chemistry textbook, written by the prolific Osei Yaw Ababio), and moved to Texas.

Unfortunately, I moved in September and missed the start of the fall semester, which starts in

---

for high-achieving students. There are typically smaller class sizes, scholarship opportunities, and study-abroad programs that are exclusively open to honors students. Honors programs may be within or outside an honors college and have students with diverse majors ranging from engineering to history. Ref: https://www.petersons.com/blog/why-you-should-enroll-in-a-college-or-university-honors-program/

August. Thus, I was forced to move my college start date to the following spring semester, which would begin in January. I used this time to ponder exactly what kind of engineering discipline I wanted to pursue and where.

Choose Wisely

The University of Texas at Arlington (UTA), which was 20 minutes from our home in Dallas, was the first choice for me and my family, primarily because of its proximity to my home. I was a fledgling 16-year-old who had just migrated across the Atlantic and needed to acclimatize to my new environment. Even though I would reside on campus, my family thought it best that I at least lived on a campus close enough to home. So, UTA was it.

My top four engineering choices were mechanical, aerospace, chemical, or petroleum engineering. Although they are all engineering disciplines, they are dissimilar.

Mechanical Engineering:

Mechanical engineers design, build and test power-producing devices, products, and equipment. They specialize in the components and equipment that may fly on aircraft or vehicles or may be used on the ground such as cooling and heating equipment, car engines, and even prosthetic devices.

Aerospace Engineering:

An aerospace engineer will focus on vehicles that fly through air or space. Aerospace engineering involves designing, building, and testing but for a more focused class of products such as aircraft, satellite, missiles, and spacecraft.

Chemical Engineering:

Chemical engineers design and conceive the processes to convert raw materials into useful products such as chemicals, fuel, drugs, and fabrics.

Petroleum Engineering:

Petroleum engineers use physics to estimate the recoverable amounts of hydrocarbons in the earth's reservoirs and devise efficient techniques to extract oil and gas from these reservoirs.

A fusion of the chemical and petroleum engineering disciplines also exists, which is petrochemical engineering. Petrochemical engineering is focused on the conversion of crude oil and petroleum into valuable and marketable products like plastics and fertilizers.

UTA didn't have a chemical or petroleum engineering program. Also, I wasn't acutely interested in either of those, but they were on my radar because I was Nigerian. Petroleum, chemical, and petro-chemical engineering had been popular choices for Nigerian engineering students since oil was discovered in the Niger-Delta region of the country in 1956. When I was deliberating on which of the disciplines to choose, Nigeria was the largest producer of crude oil on the African continent.[4] I figured it would make me successful, but I wasn't passionate about it. Thus, I was indifferent that UTA didn't have a petroleum or chemical engineering program. The decision to eliminate those engineering disciplines was easy for me.

This left me with mechanical and aerospace engineering. I also did some digging and learned that the curriculum and required coursework for these two engineering disciplines was identical for at least the first academic year. I could declare either of them as my field of study with no issues during my second year or even after. So, I declared aerospace engineering, knowing this. My father was also partial to aerospace and wanted me to be an aerospace engineer. It was easy for him to convince me.

---

[4]https://www.oecd.org/swac/publications/38798400.pdf

~~~~~~~~~~~~~~~~~~~~~~~~~~~~

**LEARN TO FLY NUGGET: SOME PEOPLE
KNOW AND PLAN OUT EVERY SINGLE
GOAL/DECISION. OTHERS DON'T.
THAT'S OKAY. WHATEVER YOU DO,
KEEP MOVING AND KNOW THAT THE
BIG PICTURE WITHOUT ALL THE
DETAILS IS STILL A PICTURE.**

~~~~~~~~~~~~~~~~~~~~~~~~~~~~

Take Useful Opportunities

After applying to UTA, I received an invitation to submit a separate application to join the Honors College (HC) at UTA. Using my college application material such as my SAT results and possibly my secondary school transcript and final exam results, the admissions office was able to calculate my secondary school Grade Point Average (GPA).

GPA was a foreign concept to me. In Nigerian secondary schools, scholastic ability was determined by your letter grades for your classes. I found it fascinating that one number between zero and four, calculated using every class you had taken, could reasonably give people a measure of how intelligent you are. *Remarkable!*

Based on the computed GPA, the university deemed me eligible for the HC. If I joined, I would need to maintain at least a 3.2 GPA out of 4.0 and I would need 24 honors credit hours[5] to graduate. The typical university course was worth either three or four credit hours. Thus, the HC credit-hour requirement implied I would need six to eight classes to graduate with the Honors Bachelor's degree in engineering. This seemed workable to me. Then I found out that the HC also had scholarships I could apply for. *Free money? Say no more.* I didn't need to be convinced any further. Applying to the HC, in addition to applying to UTA, was one of the best things I could have done.

The HC had its own building on campus, replete with reading rooms, for the very small group of admitted HC students, a tiny fraction of the university student population. In addition, the HC offered a few classes that I needed for my engineering degree. However, these classes were open only to HC students. Thus, instead of being in a Calculus class with 80 students from the general

---

[5] Honors Credit hours are obtained by taking Honors courses or by doing an extra project/homework in a non-Honors course to show that you have gone beyond the minimum required for the class.

student population, I would be in an Honors Calculus class with less than 12 HC students. There were also HC advisors, to provide additional guidance and direction, separate from the academic advisors that HC students had in their primary academic programs such as engineering or architecture. All of this was in addition to the numerous scholarship and other recognition opportunities the HC provided.

When I submitted my application to the HC, I promptly submitted the scholarship applications. Guess what? One of the things I needed for my HC Scholarship application was reference letters. I made and sent copies of them with my application. My conscientious and anxiety-ridden self would also periodically call the HC advisor to check that the HC had received my submission material and that the UTA admissions office shared what was needed with the HC. I called the HC advisor frequently to verify her receipt of my different application items and explain things she didn't ask for. At some point, she said, "Wendy, you need to calm down. You're stressing out unnecessarily. I will let you know if something is wrong or if we need any additional information."

That was my earliest indicator as a young adult that I was a worrier. After all, I was only sixteen and it really was not that serious. Thankfully, I got into the Honors college and got a scholarship. It wasn't projected to cover all my tuition and expenses, but it was a start, and I was grateful.

~~~~~~~~~~~~~~~~~~~~~~~~~~~~~~~

LEARN TO FLY NUGGET: IF YOU ARE ELIGIBLE TO JOIN AN HONORS COLLEGE IN YOUR UNIVERSITY, DO IT. IT'S A WAY FOR SMART AND HARDWORKING STUDENTS TO ACADEMICALLY THRIVE AND REALLY FOCUS ON LEARNING.

~~~~~~~~~~~~~~~~~~~~~~~~~~~~~~~

In January, four months after I arrived in Dallas, armed with my successful admission letters into UTA and the UTA HC, I visited the impressive sprawling UTA campus for orientation and met with advisors to understand my degree plan and course requirements for a mechanical and/or aerospace engineering baccalaureate degree. I was in for a shock.

The important introductory mathematics and engineering classes were offered only in the fall, August to December. I needed the first Calculus class, Introduction to Engineering, Introduction to Mechanical & Aerospace Engineering, and Design Graphics and some/all of these were offered only in the fall. This was the norm for engineering disciplines in many U.S. universities, but I didn't know this beforehand. My options were to take the core curriculum classes that were offered more routinely such as English, History, and Political Science. These core curriculum classes are required by the state of Texas for all university students in the state, regardless of chosen field of study. Paying tuition at a university to take strictly humanities courses as an engineering student felt wasteful. I was also ready for the action. So back to the drawing board I went.

There was a community college[6] close by, Mountain View Campus, that provided an affordable pathway to university and was part of the Dallas County Community College District. Mountain View was located fourteen miles Northwest of our home, and one of my sisters had gone there briefly, too. My father was also fond of community college. He routinely took graphic design classes there and loved the flexibility and tutelage he received. So, it was decided that I would go to Mountain View and

---

[6] Community or junior colleges, provide affordable post-secondary education as pathways to a four-year degree.

take some humanities courses that were required for the core engineering baccalaureate curriculum.

I visited the beautiful, large, flat-roofed Mountain View Campus building constructed over a limestone canyon, with pedestrian walkways connecting the east and west side of the campus. With only a few days until the start of classes, I quickly signed up for what was available and required to fulfill the humanities portion of my engineering degree: Macro Economics, Fundamentals of Speech, United States History, and Chemistry.

My fellow students were a diverse group of minority and adult students returning to school. Thus, the curriculum was less rigorous and more forgiving than a four-year institution to accommodate the students and enable them to learn with ease. As a result, I had a wonderful and easy semester that spring at community college. Getting all As and thus, a 4.0 GPA, was a breeze.

The fall semester at UTA wouldn't start till August, so after the spring semester at Mountain View ended in May, I promptly enrolled in more liberal arts and humanities courses. Taking an English expository writing course and a U.S. political science course in the summer, I learned how important it was to avoid plagiarism in writing and how the U.S. constitution was developed.

Armed with my 4.0 GPA from community college, SAT scores, luggage, and college readiness material, I set out for UTA almost a year after I moved to Texas. I'm being dramatic. It was only a 20-minute drive from my house in Dallas, but still, I was moving away to live on my own for the first time in my life. That was a big deal. Let's just say it got real very fast.

<u>LEARN TO FLY NUGGETS</u>

NO ONE IS EXEMPT FROM ADVERSITY. NOT A SIX-YEAR-OLD CHILD AND DEFINITELY NOT YOU. THAT'S OK. LIFE GOES ON.

IT'S NEVER TOO EARLY TO BUILD YOUR RESUME. CONSIDER ALL YOU DO IN AND OUTSIDE SCHOOL. PERHAPS YOU TUTOR MIDDLE SCHOOLERS AS A HIGH SCHOOLER. HAVE A RESUME YOU CAN BUILD ON.

DEVELOP RELATIONSHIPS WITH YOUR HIGH SCHOOL TEACHERS AND

COMMUNITY LEADERS THAT WILL ENABLE YOU TO ASK FOR RECOMMENDATION LETTERS WHEN YOU NEED THEM. SECURE THOSE LETTERS BEFORE YOU LEAVE HIGH SCHOOL IF YOU'RE MOVING AWAY.

JUST BECAUSE IT'S NOT REQUIRED DOESN'T MEAN IT'S NOT USEFUL.

SOME PEOPLE KNOW AND PLAN OUT EVERY SINGLE GOAL/DECISION. OTHERS DON'T. THAT'S OKAY. WHATEVER YOU DO, KEEP MOVING AND KNOW THAT THE BIG PICTURE WITHOUT ALL THE DETAILS IS STILL A PICTURE.

IF YOU ARE ELIGIBLE, JOIN AN HONORS COLLEGE IN YOUR UNIVERSITY. IT'S A WAY FOR SMART AND HARDWORKING STUDENTS TO ACADEMICALLY THRIVE AND REALLY FOCUS ON LEARNING.

Freshman Year (Year One)

I was now playing in the big leagues: university. Although I had declared my major as aerospace engineering, I still wasn't sure if I wanted to be an aerospace engineer or a mechanical engineer.

Mechanical engineering (ME) still held some appeal to me as it seemed broader and could open more doors. With a degree in ME, you can work in robotics, in the aerospace field, and even work in a petrochemical plant. Aerospace engineering (AE), on the other hand, was just fascinating to me. I still look up anytime I hear a plane fly overhead. I wanted to understand how a large metal tube in the sky was able to fit and transport people safely. *How magical!* Space was also cool. Everyone thinks so too, including your neighbor's daughter and your favorite preacher.

Side note: There is a difference in pressure on the top and the bottom of the wings of an airplane as it flies through air. Higher pressure on the bottom of the wings than on the top causes a pressure difference in the upwards direction. This pressure results in an upwards or lifting force that counteracts the airplane's weight and keeps it in the air. Thank you to Orville and Wilbur Wright for figuring out that the wings, and not just the engines, are crucial in enabling powered aircraft flight.

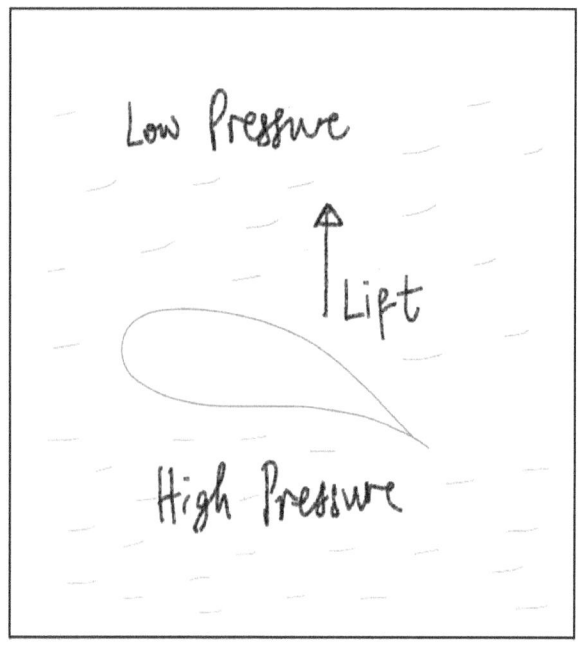

Figure 1: Cross-section of an airplane wing showing the regions of low pressure (above) and regions of high pressure (below). This pressure difference generates an upwards lifting force as a plane flies.

Even though I was Nigerian, I was also an American citizen (thanks to my Nigerian-American father). Thus, I was eligible for full-time jobs and internships in the AE field. This is more challenging for non-U.S. citizens, as most aerospace engineers work in industries that are heavily dependent on direct U.S. government funding and require U.S. citizenship, and potentially, some sort of government clearance. Had I not been American, I may have studied ME and eventually found my way into an AE career.

So, for the non-American students, please remember you don't need a baccalaureate in AE to work in an AE field, especially if the focused nature of AE may make future employment difficult. A master's degree in aerospace engineering is another option to get you into an AE field. Furthermore, computer scientists, mechanical engineers, electrical engineers, and many others are needed to make a plane fly, land a spacecraft on the moon, and place a rover on Mars.

~~~~~~~~~~~~~~~~~~~~~~~~~~~~~~~

LEARN TO FLY NUGGET: YOU DON'T NEED A BACHELOR'S DEGREE IN AEROSPACE ENGINEERING TO WORK IN THE AEROSPACE ENGINEERING INDUSTRY. COMPUTER SCIENTISTS, MECHANICAL ENGINEERS, ELECTRICAL ENGINEERS, AND MANY OTHERS ARE NEEDED TO MAKE A

PLANE FLY AND TO LAND A ROVER ON THE MOON.

~~~~~~~~~~~~~~~~~~~~~~~~~~~~~~~~

I declared my major discipline would be AE and registered for the required fall semester courses for first-year students: Calculus, Physics, Introduction to Mechanical and Aerospace (MAE) Engineering, and Introduction to Engineering. As an Honors College (HC) student, I took the Honors offerings of the Calculus and Physics courses instead of the general course offerings open to the entire university populace. The gift and curse of the small HC classes was that they had the best and brightest students from across the university and superb professors. I went from a less-challenging community college with non-traditional students to Honors classes with erudite students from all over the world. UTA was the fifth most diverse university in the nation at the time[7], so these students really were from far and wide.

My calculus professor once confided in us how delighted she was to teach this class of under 20 brilliant students. She even disclosed that all the

---

[7] https://www.theshorthorn.com/news/uta-remains-fifth-in-national-diversity/article_bf5d2d16-6639-11e5-8c90-8f53bb153305.html

mathematics professors vied to teach this coveted group each year. She would teach us Honors Calculus 1 in the fall and Honors Calculus 2 in the spring and it was perfect because I was in awe of her brilliance and teaching style.

While solving calculus problems with the class, she would occasionally get stuck on a problem that required a small simplification to complete. Stepping back with the chalk in her right hand, she would cross her left arm across her torso and peer through her glasses at the board. With her lips pursed and eyebrows furrowed in concentration, she would wonder out loud, "I just worked through this in my office. What's going on here?" Then voila, like a lightbulb went off in her head or sometimes with the help of keen student who saw that the $\sin^2 x$ in the problem can be replaced with $1 - \cos^2 x$, she would return to the board and finish. It was beautiful to witness, and in class, we worked together as a team to solve problems—students and professor. *What a truly immersive and thorough approach to learning!*

My Honors Physics 1 course was similar with an even smaller class size and a collegial atmosphere during each class session. Our professor was a renowned high-energy physicist who worked with the world's largest and most powerful particle accelerator, the Large Hadron Collider (LHC), at the

European Organization for Nuclear Research (CERN)[8]. At CERN, they would routinely accelerate particle beams, cause them to collide, and then use particle detectors to identify the subatomic particles that are produced in the collisions. *No big deal.*

Our physics professor would tell us all about his work at CERN and show us pictures in between teaching us Newton's laws and conservation of energy. I thoroughly enjoyed learning the theory and witnessing firsthand the application of fundamental physics in the discovery and understanding of our universe. Interestingly, six years later, this renowned professor would be on the team that announced the discovery of the elusive Higgs Boson, believed to give mass to even the most elementary particle and, certainly, the universe.

My introduction to MAE laboratory class was run by senior and graduate level teaching assistants. This was inspiring and I saw what I considered to be my future.

One of the teaching assistants was a brilliant and kind female senior, who patiently taught us freshmen how to design and program a mobile robot to achieve pre-defined objectives. This mobile robot

---

[8] The European Organization for Nuclear Research (CERN) located near Geneva, Switzerland, focuses on particle physics research to understand what the universe is made of and how it works: https://home.cern/about/who-we-are/our-mission

represented a robot dog that would wake up, run errands in a home, such as trash removal and clean up, and eventually return to its base charging station. The trash was a small red ball, and the home was a square region on the floor demarcated by red tape. During each class, we would build on the programming code we had written the previous week and get one step closer to a fully programmed robot that executed our imperfect designs. We would test our occasionally disloyal dog each week and nervously watch to make sure it didn't embarrass us by going rogue and exiting the square region.

My introduction to engineering class was large. It had all the engineering first years in one imposing auditorium. During class one day, professors from the various engineering departments gave brief presentations of what their engineering disciplines were. I vividly remember being enamored by the industrial engineering (IE) professor. She told us that industrial engineers made everything better and that they could work in almost any company or industry, from the Coca Cola Company to the U.S. Post Office. I learned that industrial engineers determine the best configurations for queuing that minimizes wait times for customers and clients. I wondered, "What is this cool engineering discipline that will let you work anywhere, from Disney to Apple?"

This suave professor almost influenced me to change my major from AE. She successfully convinced one of my new friends in AE to switch to IE. I still don't know exactly why I didn't switch but it's probably because I just couldn't be bothered to deal with what the change would necessitate.

~~~~~~~~~~~~~~~~~~~~~~~~~~~~~~~

LEARN TO FLY NUGGET: LETHARGY ISN'T THE WORST THING IN THE WORLD. IF YOU'RE DOING SOMETHING WELL ENOUGH AND CONSISTENTLY ENOUGH, YOU'LL FIND YOUR OWN PATH.

~~~~~~~~~~~~~~~~~~~~~~~~~~~~~~~

Ask For Help

Life was great with my honors courses and introductory engineering classes. I was still enjoying the high off my easy community college 4.0 GPA and the excitement of taking "real" engineering courses. Everything was wonderful till I took my first calculus test. I was humbled, rather quickly.

I got a 4/10. I couldn't even identify or explain what happened, but then I figured, I'll just work harder and do better next time. The next test rolled around, and I got a 6/10. At this point, I became angry with myself. I was used to doing well. I never had to study *that* hard. I excelled doing just enough. I had also just come from community college where I was one of the smartest in the class and always got above 90%. Here I was, now getting 40% - 60%, average at best. I realized after my second week in university that just enough wasn't good enough, and I would need to work a little differently.

~~~~~~~~~~~~~~~~~~~~~~~~~~~~~~~

LEARN TO FLY NUGGET: "WHEN THE GOING GETS TOUGH, THE TOUGH GET GOING" – BILLY OCEAN, BUT REITERATED MORE TIMES THAN YOU CAN IMAGINE BY MY FATHER.

~~~~~~~~~~~~~~~~~~~~~~~~~~~~~~~

The mathematics department had a learning resource center called the Math Lab where students could get additional tutoring outside of class, from senior level and graduate students. I was somewhat aware of this lab and wandered in there once during my calculus travails. It was packed with students and just seemed overwhelming to me. However, students were getting help from the skilled tutors and I liked that it was flexible with no appointment required. It didn't work for me though, as I didn't appreciate the verbal distractions between fellow students and tutors. I also didn't like that tutors had to assist multiple students in the limited time I had there. *Why couldn't they just stay with me?*

I briefly considered some sort of formal study group. But study groups can be challenging if you are not at the same skill level as the people in the study group. I once saw a dear friend studying for an exam in the MAE department laboratory with multiple groups of people. She moved from one table to another, stressed as she couldn't keep up with the pace of different groups. Imagine spending two hours of your precious time, most of which has already been claimed by engineering homework, attempting to study with people that are stressing you out even more. Two hours and you've learned nothing but how vast your ineptitude is. *What an exercise in futility and a demoralizing affair.*

~~~~~~~~~~~~~~~~~~~~~~~~~~~~~~~~

LEARN TO FLY NUGGET: EXPLORE AND FIND WHAT WORKS FOR YOU WITH STUDYING. IT MAY BE EXTRA TUTORING FROM YOUR DEPARTMENT OR A FORMAL STUDY GROUP. DON'T FORGET THE INTERNET. YOU CAN GOOGLE THE COMPLEX SUBJECT AND WATCH TUTORIAL VIDEOS ON YOUTUBE, MIT OPENCOURSEWARE, KHANACADEMY, ETC.

~~~~~~~~~~~~~~~~~~~~~~~~~~~~~~~~

I didn't want to fail with a formal study group whose members I didn't really know. However, I knew these two guys in my Honors classes. One of them was in both calculus and physics with me. The first time I noticed him was in the hallway before our first physics class. He wore a red t-shirt and brown cargo shorts and carried the largest backpack I had ever seen. I wondered why his backpack was so huge and later realized he didn't live on campus like me so he would bring all his books and textbooks each day. He probably had lunch, dinner, and a sleeping bag in there because that bag was gigantic and stuffed. I don't recall how we became friends, but we did. I didn't intentionally befriend him because of his large backpack. The friendship just happened.

The second guy was only in honors calculus with me. He didn't have a large backpack and lived in one of the apartments on campus with his older brother. Again, I don't know how we became friends, but we did. Best buds in fact.

~~~~~~~~~~~~~~~~~~~~~~~~~~~~~~~~~~~~

LEARN TO FLY NUGGET: WITH FRIENDSHIPS, YOU CAN BE STRATEGIC/INTENTIONAL, BUT ORGANIC FRIENDSHIPS ARE THE BEST. DON'T BEFRIEND SOMEONE JUST BECAUSE THEY'RE BRILLIANT. ACTUALLY, BE FRIENDS WITH THEM.

~~~~~~~~~~~~~~~~~~~~~~~~~~~~~~~~~~~~

Here's what I did with my new friends. We worked through problems together everywhere—in my room, in the library, in their apartment. We spent a lot of time together and my sisters knew their names. Unless I was eating breakfast in the cafeteria (which I ate religiously every weekday before

9:30am) or taking a nap (an almost daily after-school event), I was solving problems.

Engineering doesn't just involve studying or a reading a book cover to cover; it's about never-ending homework, solving multiple variants of different problems until you pass out and are then magically able to do it in your sleep, and putting all that problem-solving knowledge to good use when it's exam time. This sort of practice was especially important for calculus as there are tips and tricks to the most important concepts in calculus - integration and differentiation. Put simply, the former is a type of sum that enables you to add pieces an infinite number of times, while the latter enables you understand and keep track of how quickly something is changing.

A seemingly complex integration problem may just need a simplification that reduces it to a tractable trigonometric function such as sin(x), for which the integral is simply the negative of cosine(x). However, you must do many integral problems that require trigonometric simplifications so that when you see a complex trigonometric integral problem during a calculus test, you immediately know how to solve it, or you at least understand that there's a trick to simplifying it and you just need to start somewhere. The more problems you solve outside of class, the quicker you will be at solving problems during the test.

Figure 2: Photo of me in my dorm room, half-studying and half-resting on a fused study-table and bed layout

~~~~~~~~~~~~~~~~~~~~~~~~~~~~~~~~~~

LEARN TO FLY NUGGET: WHEN IN DOUBT, JUST START. THE REST WILL LIKELY FALL INTO PLACE

~~~~~~~~~~~~~~~~~~~~~~~~~~~~~~~~~~

$$\int \cos x \sin^5 x \, dx \cdots (1)$$

$$\text{Let } u = \sin x \cdots (2)$$

$$\Rightarrow du = \cos x \, dx \cdots (3)$$

Substitute (2) and (3) into (1)

$$\int \cos x \sin^5 x \, dx = \int u^5 \, du \cdots (4)$$

$$\int u^5 \, du = \frac{1}{6} u^6 + \text{constant} \cdots (5)$$

Thus,

$$\int \cos x \sin^5 x \, dx = \frac{1}{6} u^6 + \text{constant} \quad (6)$$

Substitute (2) in (6)

$$\Rightarrow \int \cos x \sin^5 x \, dx = \frac{1}{6} \sin^6 x + \text{constant}$$

Figure 3: Integral Problem involving Trigonometric Functions

After spending what felt like an infinite number of hours practicing, I got roughly 9/10 on my next test and the rest is history—mostly 9s and

10s and maybe an 8 every so often. I got an A in honors calculus 1, in honor physics 1, and in the rest of my classes. I finished my first semester in university with a 4.0 GPA, and even snagged an award, with some small funding, for being part of the small percentage of students with the highest honors in the Honors College. That induced a litany of awards that follows me to this day.

Speak Up

I overcame my first semester Honors classes with due diligence and practice, but the sailing was anything but smooth thereafter. The following semester, I got into the non-introductory and potentially challenging engineering MAE coursework. I was learning how to draw mechanical components and structures on paper and model them on a computer using ProE, a professional engineering computer-aided design tool. In another class, I was learning how to break apart a static structure, understand, and then quantify the forces and torques on it. Building upon my Honors Physics 1 foundation, this latter class involved modeling and drawing free-body diagrams[9] for entire structures,

---

[9] A free-body diagram is a pictorial representation of the forces and torques on a static or dynamic body. It is often used as a necessary

trusses, and mechanical parts. I did a lot of homework practicing how to draw these diagrams and use Newton's second law[10] to determine the forces on a body of interest.

First, you draw a free-body diagram showing the forces and their directions. Next, you identify known and unknown variables. Finally, you use Newton's second law to solve for your unknown variables using your known variables.

This non-trivial process of arriving at a final answer is the norm in engineering. The process also implies that even if you don't get the final answer correctly, you should get credit for the process. For instance, mistakenly writing down a +2 instead of -2 at the start of the process will propagate through your solution till the end. Thus, even though you will get penalized for an inaccurate final answer, you should get rewarded for thinking through and following a correct process.

However, this was not always the case for me in this class. One time, I took a test and felt good about it. To my horror, when we got our graded tests back, I got a D! When I reviewed my graded test, I felt like I didn't get enough credit for the process. I

framework for complex problems to calculate these forces and torques and associated reactions within a body.

[10] Newton's second law predicts that the net force acting on a body will equal the body's mass multiplied by its acceleration. (F = m*a).

was hurt and was sure I had been cheated. Another student, whom I knew was struggling in this and other engineering classes, got a C on the same test. My grade felt even more personal. I called my big sister, Phyllis, right after class crying, "He just does not like me because it doesn't make any sense!"

Those were fighting words to Phyllis' ears. She encouraged me to address the matter with him.

So, I sent a strongly worded email to the lecturer, letting him know that I was a member of the Honors College and a diligent student with a demonstrated record of excellence. I said, "Sir, there must be disconnect somewhere because these grades do not reflect my capabilities and efforts in your class."

I felt strongly about the issue because I knew when I didn't do well and when I did. I also took responsibility for my failures, but in this instance, I was certain that he neither graded my test equitably, nor gave me enough credit for the process of problem-solving. I had also planned to do an extra project for the class to get honors credit to meet my required honors credit hours. You had to be getting an A in the class to even be eligible to use a non-honors class for honors credit. After starting out college with a 4.0, I was adamant that this class wouldn't ruin my record. It's also easier to keep a 4.0 than to get a 4.0 from a lower GPA.

~~~~~~~~~~~~~~~~~~~~~~~~~~~~~~~~

LEARN TO FLY NUGGET: START STRONG IF YOU CAN. IT'S EASIER TO KEEP A 4.0 THAN TO GET ONE FROM A LOWER GPA.

~~~~~~~~~~~~~~~~~~~~~~~~~~~~~~~~

The lecturer responded to my strongly worded email. He said, "A student's history does not guarantee success in a new class. You must work hard and start from scratch like everybody else." He was right about the second part; however, I believe a record of excellence is an indicator of future academic success. I also felt like I was working hard and had a decent understanding of the course material.

After our next class, I approached him with my D test paper in hand, "Sir, I planned to do an extra project, as required by the Honors College, to get honors credit for your class. I can't do that unless I'm getting an A." Returning my test, I asked him if he could review it. "I understand you're a busy man with a full-time job outside of being a lecturer and you may not have had enough time to grade all tests thoroughly. Please take all the time you need and let me know if this deserves a D." He knew I had a point. Teaching was not his full-time job, and it was a large class of mechanical and aerospace engineering students. He had a lot of assignments to grade, in short order. Begrudgingly, he agreed to give mine a second look.

He never got around to reviewing that test. Instead, he gave the entire class an awesome opportunity: Complete an extra project as replacement for one test grade. My request for an extra project to fulfill my HC requirements had been the impetus for the greater good: Now, the whole class had an opportunity to scratch their lowest test score. This was fair and sufficed for me. I did my project, got an A on it, and replaced that pathetic D. I had done great on all my homework submissions, and homework accounted for 30% of the total grade. I just needed to do well on one more test and one final exam.

I aced both and got an overall A in the class. There were fellow students that did well on tests and the final exam but didn't get As. Remember, engineering coursework requires considerable homework, assigned and submitted at least once a week, sometimes multiple times a week (in the follow-on class to this, we submitted homework three times a week!). It was common for some students to avoid submitting every homework or attempting every problem on the homework because (A) homework was time-intensive and/ or (B) homework was just 30% of the overall grade. Big mistake! This mindset could easily land you 15% for your homework grades, and even if you get 100% on all your tests and final exam, you're still NOT getting an A.

In addition, most engineering professors assign final letter grades on a curve. This implies that they change the final letter grades or scores based on how the class performed overall.

Imagine: The top student in the class ends up with an 88% and this is the highest grade in the class, a high B. The professor has the discretion to add any number of percentage points, say five points, to the entire class's final grade. This brings that top student and a few others to an A and potentially improves everyone's score by a letter grade. So, you may not know what that final addition or bump will be, but you shouldn't theorize beforehand what portions of the final score breakdown you will skip or de-prioritize. This is where 3% or one homework submission makes a difference. If your final score without the curve is 73% and five percentage point gets added, you will remain a C at 78%. If that 73% was calculated with a missed 3% homework submission, that shows that one tiny homework submission was the difference between a B and a C grade for you.

One seemingly inconsequential homework could make or break your esteemed academic record. That wouldn't be me. Not this time at least.

~~~~~~~~~~~~~~~~~~~~~~~~~~~~~~~~

LEARN TO FLY NUGGET: UNDERSTAND HOW HOMEWORK PROBLEMS, TESTS, AND EXAMS ARE GRADED. DO EACH HOMEWORK PROBLEM AND SUBMIT ALL HOMEWORK ASSIGNED.

~~~~~~~~~~~~~~~~~~~~~~~~~~~~~~~~

Get Involved

During my first semester on campus, I was barely aware of and certainly not involved in any student organizations or groups. I was settling in and needed to understand the lay of the land. A college campus was new territory for me, and I needed to understand my capabilities and limitations. So, all I did was eat, study, sleep, repeat. I wanted to be an engineer and I wanted to be left alone.

However, there was a female upper class electrical engineering student who would not leave me alone. She was Nigerian too, and she would tell me, every time she saw me, about the university chapter of the Society of Women Engineers (SWE). She was the organizational public relations officer for SWE-UTA, liaising between the organization and the campus. I would often see her hanging SWE posters in the engineering buildings, general student center, and the engineering and central libraries to advertise upcoming SWE meetings and events. She was unrelenting and even once approached me in the cafeteria to emphatically inform me that she didn't see me at the last SWE meeting and was fully expecting to see me at the next one.

She said with a cheerful smile, "Wendy, I didn't see you at the last SWE meeting."

"Oh, I couldn't make it. I had to study for a test," I'd quickly reply.

"Oh no worries, we have one every month so you can just make the next one."

I'd smile and nod while thinking, *the next one? Every month? This sounds stressful. How am I ever going to get away?*

She was so persistent that I wondered if there was some hidden meaning or agenda to this invitation. *Why would anyone care about one freshman attending a meeting that had many others? I wasn't that important. Did they need me for something there? This better not be some sketchy scheme.* Alas, there was nothing to it, and she was simply looking out for me, knowing what she knew about the importance of community.

In short, I was naïve and I did not recognize the wise counsel in front of me. In the words of a well-known African proverb, "What an elder sees sitting, a young person cannot see, even if they climb a tree." I'm not saying she was an elder—I mean she was only a few years older than me. She just had more experience because she had walked my path before me. She knew how important it was for a first-year female engineering student to have a community of peers, so she deemed it her responsibility to bring me along (*Thank you, D!*).

I begrudgingly attended a meeting during the second semester of my freshman year to see what the SWE-UTA hype was about. There was free lunch during that meeting, and it was delicious. Most student organizations only had pizza at their meetings but this one would have Chinese food one meeting and Italian food another. *Yum!* More importantly, I met female students from all engineering departments and at different phases of their academic career, from freshmen to Ph.D. students. It was refreshing to be in the company of this diverse set of women and learn what they were up to. I knew instantly that I would find multiple mentors in this community, whom I could ask the tough questions like,

"Would you register for Professor A's Thermodynamics class or Professor Z's? Is it possible to graduate in four years or is that ambitious?"

~~~~~~~~~~~~~~~~~~~~~~~~~~~~~~~~

LEARN TO FLY NUGGET: YOU CAN FIND POTENTIAL MENTORS IN STUDENT ORGANIZATIONS. IT'S ONE SURE WAY TO MEET UPPER CLASSMEN THAT CAN MENTOR YOU AND PROVIDE GUIDANCE.

~~~~~~~~~~~~~~~~~~~~~~~~~~~~~~~~

Most SWE meetings would also have a female guest speaker, working in the real world, who could inspire us with her path and story, share tips for success within and outside the university campus, and share potential internship/job opportunities. I also discovered that SWE had regional and national conferences each year that students could attend and network with other students, professionals, and companies. These conferences, like many professional engineering conferences, had career fairs where you could meet a potential recruiter, face-to-face, introduce yourself, share your resume, and if they were interested, you could secure an interview on the same or next day. You could walk away from these conferences with an offer letter for an internship or job opportunity!

Learning all of this was major for me. I had previously focused only on attaining and maintaining a 4.0 GPA, but I was leaving a lot on the table by not being involved on my university campus. That was the end of my apathy towards extracurricular activities. I started to keep an eye out for potential networking opportunities, career fairs, and ways to strengthen my resume to demonstrate that I was a well-rounded student that companies would want to hire.

Luckily, at the end of the semester, elections were held for the SWE student board. I ran for a position I deemed the most important, even more important than President: the Professional Public Relations (Professional PR) officer. In this role, I would liaise between the SWE university chapter and the professional engineering world. As the Professional PR officer, I was responsible for finding and coordinating guest speakers and securing funding from industry for SWE student expenses. These expenses included travel and registration expenses to SWE local and national conferences, which were prime networking opportunities for students.

The Professional PR role was non-trivial but being the bridge to the students and the outside world meant I would meet people that could open doors for me as a rookie 17-year-old student. I got the position and was ready to roll as professional PR officer for the following academic year. I meant business.

I understand that not every university has a chapter of every organization that may be of value or interest to you. However, you can investigate what it will take to start a chapter of that organization in your university. Simply Google the national organization of interest and find a contact email or phone number to inquire how to approach starting a new section or chapter. For instance, the Society of Women Engineers directs professionals or collegians interested in starting a new section or affiliate to email membership@swe.org after which contact is established between you and SWE's Section Startup Lead. If this is too complicated for you, you can simply start your own independent organization with a small group of like-minded students. Recruit an advisor in your department who supports you and meet monthly with other students to inspire each other, advance one another, and learn from one another. You just might create the next global organization for your specific field.

~~~~~~~~~~~~~~~~~~~~~~~~~~~~~

LEARN TO FLY NUGGET: JOIN AND SERVE ON THE BOARD OF AT LEAST ONE STUDENT ORGANIZATION. IF THERE ISN'T A CHAPTER FOR A STUDENT ORGANIZATION YOU WANT IN YOUR SCHOOL, START IT AND BECOME THE FOUNDER/FOUNDING MEMBER. THIS IS A POWERFUL BOOST TO YOUR RESUME.

~~~~~~~~~~~~~~~~~~~~~~~~~~~~~

After I became the professional PR officer and before the next school year started, I had the good fortune of participating in another propitious extracurricular activity, one that propelled me to even greater heights and opened doors for me in the professional aerospace world: the Monster Diversity Leadership Program (DLP). The Monster DLP, orchestrated by Monster.com and sponsored by multiple corporate sponsors was designed to help underrepresented students in varying fields get a head start on their careers—head starts that program participants like me didn't even realize we needed till the program fell in our laps.

<u>LEARN TO FLY NUGGETS</u>

YOU DON'T NEED A BACHELOR'S DEGREE IN AEROSPACE ENGINEERING TO WORK IN THE AEROSPACE ENGINEERING INDUSTRY. COMPUTER SCIENTISTS, MECHANICAL ENGINEERS, ELECTRICAL ENGINEERS, AND MANY OTHERS ARE NEEDED TO MAKE A PLANE FLY AND TO LAND A ROVER ON THE MOON.

LETHARGY ISN'T THE WORST THING IN THE WORLD. IF YOU'RE DOING SOMETHING WELL ENOUGH AND CONSISTENTLY ENOUGH, YOU'LL FIND YOUR OWN PATH.

"WHEN THE GOING GETS TOUGH, THE TOUGH GET GOING" – BILLY OCEAN, BUT

REITERATED MORE TIMES THAN YOU CAN IMAGINE BY MY FATHER.

EXPLORE AND FIND WHAT WORKS FOR YOU WITH STUDYING. IT MAY BE EXTRA TUTORING FROM YOUR DEPARTMENT OR A FORMAL STUDY GROUP. DON'T FORGET THE INTERNET. YOU CAN GOOGLE THE COMPLEX SUBJECT AND WATCH TUTORIAL VIDEOS ON YOUTUBE, MIT OPENCOURSEWARE, KHANACADEMY, ETC.

WITH FRIENDSHIPS, YOU CAN BE STRATEGIC/INTENTIONAL, BUT ORGANIC FRIENDSHIPS ARE THE BEST. DON'T BEFRIEND SOMEONE JUST BECAUSE THEY'RE BRILLIANT. ACTUALLY BE FRIENDS WITH THEM.

WHEN IN DOUBT, JUST START. THE REST WILL LIKELY FALL INTO PLACE.

START STRONG IF YOU CAN. IT'S EASIER TO KEEP A 4.0 THAN TO GET ONE FROM A LOWER GPA.

UNDERSTAND HOW HOMEWORK PROBLEMS, TESTS, AND EXAMS ARE GRADED. DO EACH HOMEWORK PROBLEM AND SUBMIT ALL HOMEWORK ASSIGNED.

YOU CAN FIND POTENTIAL MENTORS IN STUDENT ORGANIZATIONS. IT'S ONE SURE WAY TO MEET UPPER CLASSMEN THAT CAN MENTOR YOU AND PROVIDE GUIDANCE.

JOIN AND SERVE ON THE BOARD OF AT LEAST ONE STUDENT ORGANIZATION. IF THERE ISN'T A CHAPTER FOR A STUDENT ORGANIZATION YOU WANT IN YOUR SCHOOL, START ONE AND BECOME THE FOUNDER/FOUNDING MEMBER. THIS IS A POWERFUL BOOST TO YOUR RESUME.

Sophomore Year (Year Two)

Internships and Co-Ops

Apply for a no-cost, weekend-long program and get a head start on initiating the career of your choice by networking with recruiters and learning valuable professional skills.

I blinked and re-read the email. I wasn't seeing double. It was there. An email inviting me to apply to Monster's Diversity Leadership Program (DLP), a unique summer opportunity for rising students to meet with recruiters in various industries and learn important skills for internships and job opportunities. Free! All I had to do was transport myself to the Monster DLP location and everything else would be covered.

I received this email before my first year at UTA ended and was very interested. The Monster DLP would be held across different college campuses to teach diverse undergraduate students important skills such as networking, leadership, and team building. The program would also award scholarships to exceptional students based on the involvement and leadership skills they demonstrated over the course of the program. *A complimentary event where I could learn valuable job skills and network with potential recruiters? Free housing, free food, potential scholarships? Sign me up please!*

I applied and was accepted to the Monster DLP program and discovered that not only would the program for my region be held at my university, but the participants would spend the weekend in the same on-campus residence hall I lived in. Surely this program was made for me.

That summer, I arrived at Arlington Hall on campus and was paired in a three-bedroom suite with two other students from colleges in the Southwestern U.S. We didn't know what to expect out of this program, but we were all excited. All the attendees were split into smaller groups, based on our majors, and we had interactive team building sessions, personal and professional development workshops, and even tailored resume reviews. In my cohort, I met diverse students—Jamaican, Puerto Rican, native Texan, and African American with Creole origins.

Multiple corporate sponsors were also present from different industries, including retail, information technology, finance, and aerospace. Lockheed Martin, one of the largest aerospace defense contractors for the U.S. government, was a sponsor for the event. I had heard about Lockheed Martin more times than I could count from fellow students at UTA. It was the dream company for aerospace and mechanical students alike. Even computer engineering students wanted to work there. Lockheed Martin, like the other corporate sponsors, had several representatives and recruiters dispersed within the student groups to lead and guide the exuberant horde of students through various collaborative sessions. They taught us interview skills via mock sessions and even provided individualized feedback on our resumes.

Through our interactive sessions, I met a few of the Lockheed Martin corporate representatives assigned to my group of STEM students, and earnestly engaged with them so I could get an internship, if there was any chance of that. Keeping my new SWE public relations role in mind as I networked, I also conversed with them about being potential speakers at our SWE events and providing funding for the SWE chapter to attend local and national SWE conferences. I must have made a decent impression on the Lockheed representatives, because on the final day of the program, during the close-out ceremony, I was awarded a scholarship—a scholarship I wasn't even vying for as I was focused primarily on securing an internship with Lockheed Martin. Well, I got that too through a series of unconnected events.

My genuine surprise and gratitude for the scholarship led me to individually thank the corporate representatives. During our conversations, the recruiters told me that they would share my resume with different business units of the company and would also stay in touch via email. I let them know I would be available for an internship during the following summer, right after my second year was complete.

Cooperative education[11], commonly known as co-ops, were also an option; however, I would have either taken a semester off school or worked while in school to do a co-op. A semester off can translate to a year off as most engineering classes are offered only once a year and are also prerequisite courses for other classes. So, a missed or failed class can delay graduation by a year. Although this seems like a bad deal, it may be perfect for a student who will graduate soon and has no internship or co-op experience. A co-op is also suitable for a student wanting paid employment for a longer period than just a summer. Finally, some companies offer only co-ops, as summer internships don't always provide

---

[11] Cooperative education is a student employment arrangement with a company that lasts longer than a summer internship. Unlike a summer internship in which a student briefly works for the company while on holiday and out of school, co-ops are done while school is in session.

students and employers enough time to truly work together and have a mutually beneficial experience. In any case, having at least one internship or co-op experience is critical to securing a good full-time job offer after graduating with an engineering degree. Thus, although a co-op is considerably better than nothing at all, I was itching to graduate and grow up. So, I preferred the internship route.

~~~~~~~~~~~~~~~~~~~~~~~~~~~~~~

LEARN TO FLY NUGGET: AN INTERNSHIP IS CRITICAL TO SECURING A GOOD JOB AFTER GRADUATING WITH A STEM DEGREE. DO ONE! IF YOU HAVE THE TIME, CONSIDER A CO-OP TOO.

~~~~~~~~~~~~~~~~~~~~~~~~~~~~~~

Writing Thank You Letters

After the Monster DLP program ended, I sent thank you emails to all the Lockheed Martin representatives and the other corporate sponsors I had met and developed a rapport with. I thanked them for the interview tips they gave, the resume corrections they provided, and for the $1000 scholarship I received.

Here are two emails I sent to two representatives of the corporate sponsors:

Hi Ms. Jenkins,

Thank you for that wonderful weekend at the DLP in UTA. It was a great experience, made even greater with the presence of Lockheed Martin representatives like you. I am also truly grateful for the scholarship which will definitely help out with my tuition. Thank you!

Would you please email me the contact information for the other lady that was there that weekend so I can thank her too?

I will be in touch regarding the SWE talks I had told you about. I am waiting on the President to confirm the meeting dates and then I will give you all the information.

Wendy Okolo
Monster DLP- Dallas '07 Participant
University of Texas, Arlington

Email 1

And

> *Hi Mr. Sullivan*
> *Thank you for that wonderful weekend at the*
> *Monster DLP in UTA. It was a great experience,*
> *made even greater with the presence of Lockheed*
> *Martin representatives like you. I am also truly*
> *grateful for the scholarship which will definitely help*
> *out with my tuition. Thank you!*
> *PS: I improved my resume with all the tips you*
> *gave me. It's definitely a lot better now. Thanks*
> *once again!*
>
> *Wendy Okolo*
> *Monster DLP- Dallas '07 Participant*
> *University of Texas, Arlington*

Email 2

Certain elements of the emails are identical, but each email is personalized to reflect the individual experience I had with them. The commonalities make it easier to expeditiously type and send such emails and the identifiable differences save me from embarrassment if they ever talked and realized I sent the same email to two different people.

I also thanked the program organizers and administrative staff I met during the program. These group of people work hard during such events. They typically are on their feet, barely getting a break and sometimes burning the midnight oil to ensure a seamless experience for everyone—from making sure the projectors work during a presentation to ensuring the students receive their registration materials to corralling us in an orderly fashion from lunch breaks to interview sessions. This latter group rarely hears the two words "Thank you" and would also appreciate constructive feedback on what went well and what they could improve.

Here is an email I sent to one of the program organizers:

Hi Layla Dunn,

I just wanted to say a big thank you to Monster DLP for the wonderful opportunity I was granted this past weekend. It was a very enlightening and fun weekend and I am truly grateful.

Thanks once again!
Wendy Okolo,
Dallas DLP Alumni

Email 3

In hindsight, I could have worded these emails better. Instead of greeting "Hi" a "Good afternoon," is more appropriate. There are also unnecessary qualifiers like "truly" and "definitely," but I was a teenager, and they knew it. They felt my gratitude in the emails (I hope) and that was more important than a few grammar gaffes.

~~~~~~~~~~~~~~~~~~~~~~~~~~~~~~~~~

LEARN TO FLY NUGGET: SEND THANK YOU EMAILS, EXPEDITIOUSLY—FOR THE SMALL THINGS AND FOR THE BIG THINGS. TO THE ONES YOU WANT TO IMPRESS AND TO THE ONES BEHIND THE SCENES. SAY THANK YOU!

~~~~~~~~~~~~~~~~~~~~~~~~~~~~~~~~~

Another email etiquette I would recommend for important emails is to first draft them in an offline tool like Microsoft Word or a simple Notes application. A critical email that requires me to present myself in a positive, professional light (*isn't that all of them?*) needs a little finesse and diligence.

First, I write the email in an offline tool, proofread it, then copy and paste into an email server, just in case my fingers decide to hit an absurd shortcut combination and send my incomplete email into the world. It seems time-intensive but it's not; the only extra step is the copying and pasting, and potentially a little formatting when you paste the text into the email server.

Pay Attention and Take Good Notes

A few weeks after the Monster DLP, I returned to community college in the summer to take additional core curriculum classes. After a year of taking the first two calculus classes in sequence, I now needed the third installment of calculus for my degree plan. This class, commonly called CALC III, built on the first calculus class and was also a prerequisite for the Differential Equations course I would take at UTA during my sophomore year. So, I registered for CALC III at community college and surely regretted it.

After spending a full year with the "best and brightest" at university and at the Honors College I had become accustomed to a fast-paced learning environment with traditional students and professors. As described in Chapter 2, community college classes were geared towards enabling non-traditional and returning students to succeed, sometimes with a much slower learning pace than a four-year institution. I didn't mind that at all. The challenge was that the extremely slow pace of the CALC III class I was in could prevent us from covering the gamut of the CALC III syllabus. The patient professor, who was also advanced in his years, made sure to thoroughly work through every problem on the board. By that, I mean he would painstakingly write out each step of the solution to every problem we solved, to the very final answer. This meant that instead of quickly working through perhaps fifteen different types of CALC III problems, we would thoroughly work through only four or five.

I was frustrated and nervous that we wouldn't cover the entire syllabus of CALC III. I was right, we didn't. We learned partial derivatives and how to differentiate functions of multiple variables. We barely studied cylindrical co-ordinates as we mostly stayed in the standard Cartesian three-dimensional co-ordinate system – x, y, and z, represented using i, j, and k vector notation. I surely didn't learn the spherical co-ordinate system, nor did I learn how to convert from spherical to Cartesian co-ordinate frames. Good luck understanding what a Lagrange multiplier was and how to optimize a function to a given constraint. However, I got my A and the non-traditional students in the class at least got a rudimentary understanding of CALC III. So, I guess that was still a win—a win I paid dearly for when I started Differential Equations the following semester at UTA.

~~~~~~~~~~~~~~~~~~~~~~~~~~~~~~~~~~

LEARN TO FLY NUGGET: DON'T GET COMFORTABLE IN YOUR STEM COURSES IF YOU'RE AT A COMMUNITY COLLEGE. GOOGLE AND USE THE SYLLABI OF THE CORRESPONDING UNIVERSITY COURSES TO GUIDE YOUR STUDYING SO THAT YOU CAN BE ON-PAR WITH YOUR PEERS WHEN YOU TRANSITION TO UNIVERSITY.

~~~~~~~~~~~~~~~~~~~~~~~~~~~~~~~~~~

I enjoyed Differential Equations, and I liked my professor. It was a full class, but I always sat in the first two rows, listened to everything he said, and asked questions if I missed even a word. If you pay undivided attention in class, it's easy for you to go home and simply do the homework problems, as required for engineering and most STEM degrees. If you don't pay attention, you must go home, relearn what was taught in class using your textbooks or other resources, and then do the homework problems. This is stressful and time-consuming. It ultimately results in students doing various permutations and combinations to quantify which homework assignments to skip for what classes, simply because they are overwhelmed. Also, this mode of operation leaves little room for extracurricular activities, which are important for your well-being and even for your academic success.

I had such a fear of missing anything in my brain-intensive classes that if I ever zoned out, I'd zone back in immediately and ask the professor to please paraphrase. One time, my Differential Equations professor said something that I didn't give myself time to process. Not wanting to miss a concept that could show up on a test, I immediately asked him a trite follow-up question. When he replied to me with the professor equivalent of "duh," I was mortified. He caught a glimpse of my disappointed, embarrassed face and kindly clarified my premature confusion. This interchange exemplifies how physically close I sat to the action: My professors and I could read each other's non-verbal cues. When they cracked jokes that weren't funny, I'd smile or laugh (only if it was truly funny), because I knew they were trying up there.

Paying undivided attention is also a respectful thing to do. Nothing tangibly prevents you from texting or talking to a fellow student throughout the lecture, but professors see everything and most times, say nothing. Be kind and wise. It defeats the purpose of learning if you simply come to class to mark attendance, do things unrelated to the course (like social media), and then go back home to relearn what your professor just taught. The same applies to distance learning. If you turn off your camera and stay on TikTok throughout your online class, you must still spend additional time afterwards relearning what has just been taught. That is hustling backwards.

~~~~~~~~~~~~~~~~~~~~~~~~~~~~~~

LEARN TO FLY NUGGET: SIT CLOSE TO THE FRONT, LEARN TO LISTEN, BE KIND AND RESPECTFUL. YOUR PROFESSORS CAN SEE EVERYTHING. EVEN IF YOU ARE TAKING CLASSES ONLINE, PUT YOUR PHONE AWAY AND LISTEN.

~~~~~~~~~~~~~~~~~~~~~~~~~~~~~~

In my situation, I did have to spend time outside the class learning the CALC III content we skipped in community college. I needed to apply the CALC III knowledge to applications in the Differential Equations course. I didn't appreciate the relearning, but I had no choice if I wanted to get an A in Differential Equations. This is why I recommend (A) taking primarily core curriculum classes in community college like History, English, Political Science, that have no bearing on your engineering or STEM classes or (B) ensuring you do the research to confirm that the content, delivery, timeline for the STEM class in community college aligns with your university. I didn't.

How would you do that research anyway? Perhaps you could review the syllabus of the class and meet with the community college professor beforehand to understand what is covered. Another option is to ask your academic advisor at university what they would recommend or if there is a specific community college or professor whose tutelage they are familiar with. Finally, don't forget about senior students, a hidden trove of resources and knowledge. They've recently gone through what you're going through and will surely tell it like it is. But how does a freshman/sophomore meet upper class students with similar majors? You could sign up for a mentoring program that pairs upper class students with lower class students? I tried that my freshman year, but I never heard from my mentor and promptly forgot I was even assigned one. However, I have learned that the best mentoring relationships are the ones that form organically and develop into a true friendship. Extracurricular activities can help you form and develop these friendships.

As professional PR officer for the university chapter of SWE, I was part of the board members that comprised of other elected officers such as the president, vice-president, secretary, and treasurer, etc. This board and other SWE members who attended our meetings were at varying levels of their undergraduate studies. Thus, it was easy to meet and form organic relationships with upperclassmen whom I could ask the right questions like "Do you have any recommendations regarding taking CALC III in community college?"

Remember I said extracurricular activities can be vital to your academic success? Well meeting mentors via student organizations and simply being part of a community of like-minded individuals can be a springboard to scholastic success. In my case, I should have asked a senior student and SWE member about the CALC III class before I registered for it, but I was new to the organization, barely knew anyone, and didn't think to ask.

~~~~~~~~~~~~~~~~~~~~~~~~~~~~~~~

LEARN TO FLY NUGGET: IF YOU'RE UNSURE ABOUT YOUR CLASS SCHEDULE OR CONSIDERING TAKING CLASSES AT ANOTHER SCHOOL, FIRST SEEK THE OPINION OF YOUR ADVISOR AND A SENIOR STUDENT.

~~~~~~~~~~~~~~~~~~~~~~~~~~~~~~~

Time Optimization

All SWE members were required to spend a minimum number of hours each week in the SWE office. Our small office in the main engineering building was equipped with two brown adjacent tables, cushioned chairs, a desktop computer, a small sofa, and folders and boxes with SWE-related content that went back several years. During my office hours, I would provide information to potential members who sometimes wandered down our hallway seeking information. I would also conduct SWE professional PR business such as contacting corporate organizations to solicit sponsorship for students to attend local and national SWE conferences and emailing potential guest speakers to attend our meetings and inspire the students. I was also responsible for planning and coordinating tours for our students to engineering companies and preparing budget estimates and pledge proposal documents for our corporate sponsors. Now this may all seem like a chore and a diversion from doing schoolwork, but here's why it wasn't.

On-campus housing was located at the perimeters of the university campus, a distance away from the academic buildings where classes were conducted. Thus, going from my residence hall to either the MAE building, or the main engineering building was a ten-to-fifteen-minute walk. Students would try to register for classes that ran one after the other, but options were generally limited. You were more likely find two classes on Mondays, Wednesdays, and Fridays from 9-9:50 and 11-11:50 and the other two classes on Tuesday and Thursdays from 8-9:20 and 11-12:20. Thus, every day of the week, there would be time between classes where you had to find a place to simply wait it out.

Some students would simply sit at the tables in the common areas while others would go to the library. Some students would go to the student center and engage with other students across the university, and a brave few would make the arduous trek to the residence hall and back. I had all these options, but I also had the option of a mostly unoccupied private office in the main engineering building where I could study, do homework, conduct SWE duties, or even take a quick nap on the couch. Thus, my time in the academic buildings was optimized, stress-free, and mostly productive. I would return to my residence hall only if it was crucial or after my last class of the day. No walking back and forth unnecessarily. *Life was good!*

~~~~~~~~~~~~~~~~~~~~~~~~~~~~~~~~~~~

LEARN TO FLY NUGGET: OPTIMIZE YOUR TIME AND BE PRODUCTIVE IN BETWEEN CLASSES. THIS GIVES YOU MORE TIME FOR REST, RELAXATION, AND ENJOYMENT.

~~~~~~~~~~~~~~~~~~~~~~~~~~~~~~~~~~~

Professional Development

That fall semester, I and a few other students travelled to Nashville, Tennessee for the SWE

National Conference. It was the Monster DLP on steroids! There were small meeting rooms where sessions were conducted by various people in industry, government, and academia on different topics of relevance to female engineers. There was a big hall for keynote speeches, plenary talks, and panel discussions for the larger SWE audience. Most importantly, there was a huge exposition hall where the career fair was held with multiple companies, universities, and government agencies showcasing their cool technologies, giving out the best freebies, and engaging with potential employees who were interested in an internship or full-time opportunity. This was where the magic happened.

Armed with my SWE registration bag slung over my left shoulder, paper folder containing twenty printed copies of my one-page resume clutched in my left hand, I walked into the exposition hall and proceeded to engage with any company that looked even remotely "aerospacey." I'd hover around their booth and wait for a recruiter to become available, stick out my right hand for a firm handshake and say, "My name is Wendy Okolo and I'm an aerospace engineering student at the University of Texas at Arlington. I would like an internship next summer and here is a copy of my resume for your review." I would then proceed to highlight key bullets on the resume, and they would in turn share internship opportunities with instructions on how to secure them. These instructions typically included a specific website with a passcode for SWE conference attendees only. Most of the companies and representatives were available to interview potential students during the conference and I secured a few interviews while I was there.

A magnet for many conference attendees, the large, glorious, and imposing Lockheed Martin exhibit station was easy to find. The exhibit had models of different aircraft on display, screens showing the company's warfighter capabilities, various paraphernalia describing the multiple career opportunities within Lockheed Martin, and souvenirs that students and professionals alike fawned over. I waited for a recruiter so I could stick my right hand out for a handshake and begin my spiel when I saw a recruiter I already knew! I had met her at the Monster DLP.

She remembered me and I struck up a conversation with her, shared my resume once more, and grabbed a few freebies. She told me that she and the other recruiters I had met at Monster DLP were already working to find me an internship with Lockheed Martin. However, the exact location and specific business unit were unknown. I thanked her for the update but still conducted the interviews I had with the other companies. I also honored the invitations to hospitality suites[12] that I had received from other companies. My first SWE conference was wonderful, and I left the conference positive that I would receive a few internship offers and get to play in the real aerospace world.

~~~~~~~~~~~~~~~~~~~~~~~~~~~~~~~

LEARN TO FLY NUGGET: UNDERGRADUATE STUDENT RESUMES SHOULD TYPICALLY BE ONE PAGE LONG. HAVE 20-25 HARD COPIES OF YOUR RESUME JUST IN CASE ELECTRONIC COPIES ARE NOT ACCEPTED OR YOU ARE UNABLE TO PRINT ONSITE AT A CONFERENCE.

~~~~~~~~~~~~~~~~~~~~~~~~~~~~~~~

Here is my first ever resume, which is obviously paltry and reeks of inexperience. Although it is clearly deficient in relevant aerospace

---

[12] Hospitality suites are intimate receptions/rooms hosted by individual companies to provide additional networking and discussion between potential employees and recruiters in a more relaxed setting.

engineering experience and contains unnecessary phrases instead of the quick bullet points a recruiter wants to see, the programming, software, and operating system proficiencies, coupled with the high GPA in boldface is an indicator of potential technical competence in a non-academic environment. The non-relevant work experience in sales and clerical duties demonstrates consistency and possibly a decent work ethic. Finally, the extracurricular activities portend that I can work well with multiple people on a team to achieve a common goal.

Recruiters and hiring managers look out for these skills, very quickly, when they review a resume. Thus, even though you may lack experience in a specific field, think deeply about the non-obvious skills you have developed that will enable you to succeed in that field and highlight them concisely.

Wendy A. Okolo
insert complete mailing address
*insert working phone number *
insert professional email address e.g. FirstnameLastName@emailprovider.com

Objective   To employ my scholastic and personal skills at an internship.

Education   **University of Texas at Arlington**   **GPA: 4.0**
                         Aerospace Engineering Undergraduate Sophomore

Computer Skills   **Software** – I have worked extensively with MS Word, Excel,
                         PowerPoint, & Pro E.
                         Operating Systems – I have over eight years of experience with
                         MS DOS, Windows 95, 98, XP.
                         Programming – I have a basic knowledge of the C program.

Experience   **Incept**
                         Receptionist   January '06 – Present
                         Scheduling appointments, handling mail, and simple bookkeeping.
                         Lumog
                         Salesperson   February '05 – February '05
                         Company promotional store-to-store salesperson that convinced buyers
                         to purchase perfumes at the Lumog stands, resulting in earnings of over
                         $1000 in one week.

Activities   **Society of Women Engineers (Professional PR)**   2007 – Present
                         Act as an agent between engineering companies and the organization
                         and invite industry personnel to speak at general meetings.
                         UTA HOSTS (Mentor)   2007 – Present
                         Mentor female engineering freshmen and assist in their assimilation of
                         the university; thereby increasing minority participation in technical
                         fields.
                         African Students Organization (ASO)   2006 – Present
                         Member of the dance team which provides entertainment at fundraisers,
                         competitions, and other events.
                         St. Charles Choir   2001 – 2005
                         Member of the youth and adult choir at St. Charles Borromeo Catholic
                         Church

Honors & Awards   **National Dean's List**   2007
                         Award received by ½ of 1% of the nation's college students.
                         Honors College UTA   2006 – Present
                         One of 700 students out of 19,000 undergraduates in the university.
                         National Society of Collegiate Scholars   2007 – Present
                         President's Honor Roll (Mountainview College)   2006

If you need additional help with writing your resume, see if your school has a career center that will help you refine your resume. Even local libraries have job search tips and resume workshops with experts that can help. Finally, you can simply Google a resume sample for someone in your field and at your level of study. You can use the sample as a guide or even use ChatGPT to write your resume. However, ensure that you tailor your resume based on the samples you find. Please don't copy and paste and keep the creator's email in your resume. Finally, pore over that resume and remove any grammatical errors. My next resume iteration contained the term "flow blow diagrams" instead of "flow block diagrams" and a recruiter promptly identified it to my chagrin. Don't be me. Proofread to the maximum!

Paying for Training and Development

When I returned from the SWE conference, I prepared and sent a pledge proposal document in my capacity as professional PR, to a Lockheed Martin representative I had a met at the Monster DLP, asking for funds to reimburse the students who had attended the SWE conference. As professional PR officer, I was responsible for finding funding mechanisms for students to defray our professional development costs such as conference attendance. I was successful; however, the costs were not exorbitant. We shared a hotel room during the conference, had most meals provided during the conference, and simply had to independently cover airfare and registration costs, which are typically minimal for student attendees.

~~~~~~~~~~~~~~~~~~~~~~~~~~~~~~~

LEARN TO FLY NUGGET: IT'S NOT ALWAYS EXPENSIVE TO ATTEND A NETWORKING CONFERENCE AND THE COSTS YOU INCUR CAN SOMETIMES BE COVERED INTERNALLY BY THE UNIVERSITY OR EXTERNALLY BY AN ORGANIZATION. PLEASE ASK (MENTORS, PROFESSORS, ADVISORS, AND COMPANY REPRESENTATIVES) AND ASK POLITELY!

~~~~~~~~~~~~~~~~~~~~~~~~~~~~~~~

See below for my modified pledge proposal letter requesting funding. Feel free to modify and use it for a potential sponsor to help defray costs associated with your professional development.

Ensure that your organization complies with all applicable federal and state tax laws and operates exclusively on a not-for-profit basis. Funding should not be used to generate income for individuals and/or the organization. When in doubt, ask a qualified tax professional.

October 29, 20XX

Nia Jenkins,
Campus Recruiting Representative
Lockheed Martin Corporation

Dear Ms. Jenkins,

The Society of Women Engineers student chapter at The University of Texas at Arlington (SWE UTA) encourages women to achieve full potential in careers as engineers and leaders, expand the image of the engineering profession as a positive force in the quality of life, and demonstrate the value of diversity. Two ways we accomplish our goals are by reaching out to middle and high school students and enlightening them about engineering, and by sending our student members to the SWE National Conference.

SWE's intentions with the outreach program are to go to the schools and encourage young girls to consider technical majors upon admission to universities. Educational brochures and pamphlets, and prizes for the activities such as T-shirts, and hats, would be given out to these girls and I have included an estimate for the outreach program in the breakdown of costs below.

Furthermore, Lockheed Martin is a major sponsor of the SWE National Conference and so as a company, it is familiar with all the amazing opportunities the conference provides in areas relevant to the modern engineer. This year's National Conference, SWe-XX, Women in Tune with Technology, was held on October 25-27 in Nashville, Tennessee. Students had the opportunity to attend the Career Fair and Exhibits, workshops focusing on Professional Development, and networking events, while preparing them for their future; this conference was a great opportunity for our members.

Please help us in our efforts by making a tax-deductible, monetary donation. Your donation will get SWE UTA members reimbursed for participating in the National Conference. I have also included a breakdown in cost for the students which is approximately $1875.00.

We would really appreciate any assistance you can provide for SWE UTA. Thank you for your time and

> *consideration. Please contact me if you have any questions and would be willing to help us in any way.*
>
> *Sincerely,*
> *Wendy A. Okolo*
> *Professional Public Relations Officer*
> *Society of Women Engineers, U.T. Arlington*

Two months after the conference, I was being courted by three aerospace companies for an internship position after my sophomore year. It was not an easy decision, but I chose Lockheed Martin. I had developed a longer relationship with them and knew their recruiters and a few employees personally. The internship was in Houston, Texas, and it was going to be my first foray into the professional aerospace world. I was thrilled! However, before the school year ended, I had a slight hiccup.

Dealing With Everyday Challenges

I lived with two randomly assigned students in the residence hall. My first-year roommates were relatively quiet, and we all had independent non-conflicting schedules. All social gatherings were conducted primarily outside our suite. So, at nighttime, we were mostly in our rooms except for the occasional activity in the shared restroom, sink area, or kitchenette. One of them even had a part-time job, so sleep was important to her. Although we had different majors with varying levels of commitment/homework intensity, we were on the same page.

My second year was a different story. Things started out well enough but by the second semester, my living situation became untenable. My two roommates became close friends, which was all well and good. However, our suite became the hangout spot.

I shared a wall with the living room; thus, I could hear any loud activities. I would occasionally be woken up in the middle of the night to a ruckus and it was infuriating. Once, I made the mistake of coming out of my bedroom to ask if they could keep it down. It was 2 a.m. and I had an early class. That made things significantly worse, and the noise and passive aggressiveness increased intensely. I didn't realize I could ask the housing staff for help, and I didn't consider moving to a different unit. I just managed the unfortunate situation for weeks until they got tired and one of them moved out.

Even though things got better, I was done sharing my space and having no control over what happened where I lived. *The quality of sleep I got at night should not be dependent on whether my roommates wanted to hang out late or wanted to mess with me that day.* I was sick of it and determined not to share a suite the following semester. I wanted an apartment to myself.

I told my family and was promptly forbidden from doing such! My sister, Jennifer, had watched way too many crime shows featuring a poor lady who lived alone and ended up in distress. They all deemed it unsafe for a young eighteen-year-old girl to live alone in an apartment, whether off-campus or on-campus. I was outnumbered and had to think fast.

Serendipitously, the timing coincided with a call for new resident assistants[13] (RAs) for the following school year. I did some research and found out that RAs had their own spaces (private rooms and private bathrooms) within the residence halls and didn't have to share or deal with shenanigans like I had. They also got a free meal plan and reduced housing rates. *Really? This sounded like enjoyment.*

I applied and prepared for the two-part interview that consisted of (A) a semi-formal question and answer session with the Apartment & Resident Life staff members (RAs and residence directors) and (B) an experiential session where I

---

[13] A resident assistant is a student who lives in a residence hall with other students and assists with their transition into university, conflict resolution, and rule enforcement, while responding to complaints, emergencies, and other requests.

would be thrust into a simulated but high-stress experience that would require leadership and quick thinking. I aced the semi-formal question and answer session and prepared for the complex second half of the interview.

We were split into groups and placed in varying scenarios. My group of three applicants were called into a room with four RAs, acting as uncooperative students that were partying, drinking, and disturbing the peace. With no prior experience, were asked to end it immediately by asking the non-resident students to leave and gathering relevant information for documentation. If we couldn't, we had to simulate escalating the situation to a residence hall director or calling our campus police. *What had I gotten myself into?* I wondered if I really needed that private room and bathroom. *Wendy, are you sure you can't manage your living situation?* By the special grace of God, I pulled myself together and worked with my fellow RA aspirants to deescalate the situation. I passed the interview and was stoked. My family was reassured, and I was going to be an RA in the newest residence hall on campus. *Wonderful!*

~~~~~~~~~~~~~~~~~~~~~~~~~~~~~

LEARN TO FLY NUGGET: DO HARD THINGS. PERSISTING THROUGH NON-

SCHOLASTIC RIGORS TEACHES DISCIPLINE THAT WILL HELP YOU PERSEVERE THROUGH ACADEMIC CHALLENGES.

~~~~~~~~~~~~~~~~~~~~~~~~~~~~~~~~~~~

At the end of the semester, I traded in my professional SWE PR position for president, attaining a different set of SWE responsibilities for the next school year. With my new RA position secured, SWE president role attained, summer internship locked in, and another 4.0 GPA, I finished my semester on a high note. I packed my bags, loaded up my 1997 Toyota RAV4 and began the four-hour drive to Houston, Texas for my summer internship. The summer was going to be "lit," literally, since the air conditioning in my car didn't work and Houston summer temperatures are over 100 degrees Fahrenheit). Oh well, I was still excited.

LEARN TO FLY NUGGETS

AN INTERNSHIP IS CRITICAL TO SECURING A GOOD JOB AFTER GRADUATING WITH A STEM DEGREE. DO ONE! IF YOU HAVE THE TIME, CONSIDER A CO-OP TOO.

SEND THANK YOU EMAILS, EXPEDITIOUSLY, FOR THE SMALL THINGS AND FOR THE BIG THINGS. TO THE ONES YOU WANT TO IMPRESS AND TO THE ONES BEHIND THE SCENES. SAY THANK YOU!

DON'T GET COMFORTABLE IN YOUR STEM CLASSES IF YOU'RE AT A COMMUNITY COLLEGE. GOOGLE AND USE THE SYLLABI OF THE CORRESPONDING UNIVERSITY COURSES TO GUIDE YOUR STUDYING SO THAT YOU CAN BE ON-PAR WITH YOUR PEERS WHEN YOU TRANSITION TO UNIVERSITY.

SIT CLOSE TO THE FRONT, LEARN TO LISTEN, BE KIND AND RESPECTFUL. YOUR PROFESSORS CAN SEE EVERYTHING. EVEN IF YOU ARE TAKING CLASSES

ONLINE, PUT YOUR PHONE AWAY AND LISTEN.

IF YOU'RE UNSURE ABOUT YOUR CLASS SCHEDULE OR CONSIDERING TAKING CLASSES AT ANOTHER SCHOOL, FIRST SEEK THE OPINION OF YOUR ADVISOR AND A SENIOR STUDENT.

OPTIMIZE YOUR TIME AND BE PRODUCTIVE IN BETWEEN CLASSES. THIS GIVES YOU MORE TIME FOR REST, RELAXATION, AND ENJOYMENT.

UNDERGRADUATE STUDENT RESUMES SHOULD TYPICALLY BE ONE PAGE LONG. HAVE 20-25 HARD COPIES OF YOUR RESUME JUST IN CASE ELECTRONIC COPIES ARE NOT ACCEPTED OR YOU ARE UNABLE TO PRINT ONSITE AT A CONFERENCE.

IT'S NOT ALWAYS EXPENSIVE TO ATTEND A NETWORKING CONFERENCE AND THE COSTS YOU INCUR CAN SOMETIMES BE COVERED INTERNALLY BY THE UNIVERSITY OR EXTERNALLY BY AN

ORGANIZATION. PLEASE ASK (MENTORS, PROFESSORS, ADVISORS, AND COMPANY REPRESENTATIVES) AND ASK POLITELY!

DO HARD THINGS. PERSISTING THROUGH NON-SCHOLASTIC RIGORS TEACHES YOU DISCIPLINE THAT WILL HELP YOU PERSERVERE THROUGH ACADEMIC CHALLENGES.

Junior Year (Year Three)

No Pressure

An actual spacecraft that would carry real living human astronauts away from the earth and to the moon: Its name was Orion, and it was NASA's replacement for the Apollo[14] spacecraft that successfully landed the first humans on the moon in 1969. That's what I would work on. *No pressure.*

Orion was the exploration vehicle that would not only take the astronauts to space and the moon but would sustain them during travel and provide safe re-entry to earth, considering the high velocities of space return and the harsh vibration and thermal environments experienced during reentry. *Who trusted me to be even the tiniest little bit responsible for this vehicle that was being designed to carry astronauts away from and back to the earth?*

---

[14] The Apollo program, through multiple missions utilizing an Apollo spacecraft and space launch system, took humans beyond the Earth's orbit and landed the first humans on the moon. It enabled an understanding of the moon, its history, and geological composition and spurred multiple advances in research and technology.

Figure 4: Apollo Spacecraft Crew Module[15]

My work location was a seven-minute drive from NASA's Johnson Space Center (JSC) and Lockheed Martin was a primary contractor and provider of space services for JSC. In fact, Lockheed Martin, simply referred to as Lockheed, was the prime contractor for the development of Orion. Both JSC and Lockheed were twenty-five miles south of downtown Houston, Texas in Houston's Bay Area.

15

https://www.nasa.gov/sites/default/files/images/618811main_1969-04-01_full.jpg

Figure 5: Rendering of the Orion Spacecraft

Luckily, I had free room and board in Galveston, TX with my sister who was in medical school in Galveston. With no traffic, I could make the 31-mile commute in 40 minutes. However, that was rare, as Houston is notorious for traffic. Knowing this, I left early enough on my first day because I refused to be the tardy new intern. I arrived right on time dressed in a long-sleeved dress shirt, black slacks, and a pair of shiny black low-heeled shoes.

One of my first stops was the badging office where I received my Lockheed Martin identification. *How official!* I also got a NASA identification card since I was working on a NASA contract and might have to visit NASA JSC during the internship. Then I went to the Human Resources (HR) office where I filled out additional paperwork and received necessary orientation information. Finally, my HR representative called my manager to pick me up and show me to my cubicle and team.

My team was called the Requirements Management Office (RMO) under the Systems Engineering[16] and Integration division. Members of the RMO, interns included, worked in individual cubicles on the second floor of the building. My manager showed me to my cubicle, and I was thoroughly pleased. *Eek! My own space?* I mildly wondered how I would arrange my things on my desk as I laid my bag and folders down. I corralled my wandering mind back and made my way to my manager's office, where she gave me an overview of the RMO.

The RMO, a critical facet of Orion's development, documented, organized, traced, and prioritized requirements for the components, systems, and interfaces of the vehicle. Just like the name implies, a requirement describes in clear

---

[16] Systems engineering is a multidisciplinary engineering discipline that works with other engineering groups to ensure that the design and development of a complex functional system is seamless and well-integrated. Simply, system engineers make sure that the different engineers talk to one another, so that Engineer A doesn't design a square bolt for a round hole designed by Engineer B.

qualitative terms the purpose and constraints of a component, subsystem, system, or even system of systems. The RMO also tracked any changes to requirements and communicated them to relevant stakeholders within and outside the company.

I scribbled in my notepad, what my manager told me about the RMO and our Lockheed Martin business unit. She then proceeded to introduce me to all the members of my team—engineers and administrative staff included. I struggled to remember all the names and worried that I would have to ask them again the next day. So, after meeting everyone, I noted identifying characteristics with the names in my book. However, our cubicles had name tags so that may have been unnecessary. *Oh well.*

~~~~~~~~~~~~~~~~~~~~~~~~~~~~~~~~~~

LEARN TO FLY NUGGET: GIVE A FIRM HANDSHAKE AND LOOK PEOPLE IN THE EYE WHEN YOU ARE INTRODUCED. NOTE ANY IDENTIFYING CHARACTERISTICS WITH THE NAMES AFTER YOU MEET THEM SO YOU CAN REMEMBER THEIR NAMES. USE THEIR NAMES IN

CONVERSATION WITH THEM. BE PRESENT.

~~~~~~~~~~~~~~~~~~~~~~~~~~~~~~~~~

Finally, I was introduced to the most inspiring mentor who laid out my roles and responsibilities with some starting tasks for me. She gave me some Microsoft Excel spreadsheets that described requirements my student-brain found remarkable: from high-level requirements that stated the ultimate goals of Orion such as landing on the moon, to low level requirements that described weight limits for nuts and bolts, to software performance requirements that specified minimum computing capabilities required.

Part of my duties involved transferring requirement specifications from a cloud-based database to an offline database, and vice versa. I learned that with professional work your backup should have a backup. In addition, you may create work on your local computer but need to access it from another computer in the future. Your teammate could also want to access that work from their computer, hence the need for an online cloud-based architecture that's accessible by multiple users.

Some of the requirements were also outdated or needed additional specifications. Thus, I needed to contact the subject-matter experts (SMEs) outside the RMO to get updates on the missing pieces. This was a non-trivial task because these SMEs were predictably busy with design and development; clarifying specifications to an intern in the RMO was low on their priority list. I had to be persistent, polite, and tactful.

My mentor was also there to guide me while also challenging me to independently solve challenges she deemed I could handle. She would purse her lips and ask, "Well, what do you think?" anytime she thought I could figure it out. The first time it happened, I was disconcerted but quickly realized it comes with the territory of the professional work environment where there isn't always a right or wrong answer, unlike in school. Multiple solutions and approaches can create desirable outcomes.

Although I was an intern, I was nonetheless part of a team and had to understand the roles of my teammates and their progress towards the RMO goals. Their updates could help me with my work and vice versa, so we had a steady cadence of meetings where we all shared our work. Meetings are an integral part of full-time work, and this was new to me as a student who only had attended SWE meetings once or twice a month. Now I had multiple meetings in one day with no breaks to nap in the SWE office, no opportunity to go back to my dorm to watch *Family Guy*, and no calling my friends or family to talk on the phone.

Being mentally alert for eight hours a day took some getting used to, and I would sometimes struggle to stay awake during these meetings. So, I started to take good notes and write down things that were said in these meetings, whether I considered them important or not. I wrote to keep myself alert; however, I failed sometimes and nodded off on a few occasions. I also broke up my day with a snack break, lunch break, or a quick social or technical chat at another intern's or coworker's cubicle.

~~~~~~~~~~~~~~~~~~~~~~~~~~~~~~~~~~~

LEARN TO FLY NUGGET: TAKE NOTES DURING MEETINGS TO KEEP YOURSELF ALERT. IF POSSIBLE, EAT LUNCH OUTSIDE AND/OR TAKE QUICK WALKS OUTSIDE IN THE FRESH AIR TO BREAK UP YOUR DAY. CAFFEINE ALSO HELPS. IF YOU FALL ASLEEP DURING A MEETING, GIVE YOURSELF SOME GRACE. IT'S OK.

~~~~~~~~~~~~~~~~~~~~~~~~~~~~~~~~~~~

Interns also got multiple tours and professional development opportunities within and outside Lockheed. I once got to tour a docking[17] simulation facility where I practiced docking the Orion Crew Exploration Vehicle with the International Space Station.[18] I failed woefully at that simulation and gained an even greater appreciation for astronauts who performed such high-risk maneuvers in space with little to no help from our atmosphere, which provides beneficial resistance. I also went to NASA JSC to visit renowned locations such as the Mission Control Center where flight directors and other system leads communicated in near real-time with astronauts in space, on the ISS, and even the moon in the 1960s and 1970s. I visited the Neutral Buoyancy Laboratory (NBL), a large indoor swimming pool created to simulate a microgravity environment and prepare astronauts for working in space. Astronauts would practice performing extravehicular activities in the NBL as they would have to on a real mission.

---

[17] Docking is the physical joining of two separate and independent free-flying spacecraft.

[18] The International Space Station (ISS) is a large modular free-flying spacecraft built by multiple space agencies to house astronauts and provide a space for scientific and educational research.

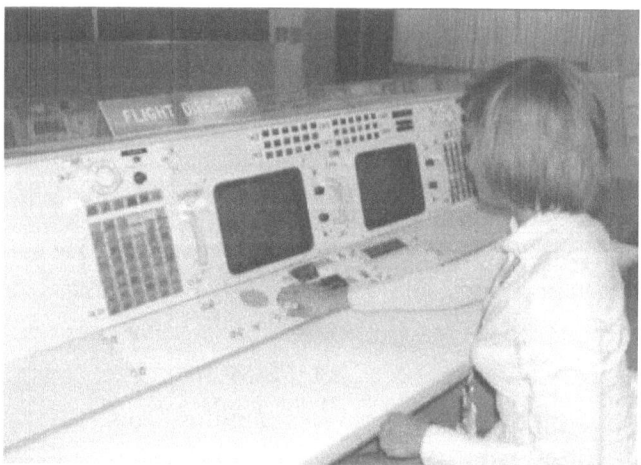

Figure 6: Photo of me in the old Mission Control Center (MCC) at NASA Johnson Space Center (JSC)

Get Social

We also had sessions where guest speakers and panelists from all ranks within the company shared their journeys, advice, and work with us, from executive vice presidents overseeing different business units, to early-career employees within the first three years of their careers. These were amazing opportunities to learn about the different facets of the company, but they were also great visibility opportunities for interns who were bold enough to stand out, ask questions, and introduce themselves to these seasoned leaders. However, there was another hidden trove of resources to learn more about the company that was often overlooked by many interns, me included: other interns!

We had an internal organization called Lockheed Entertainment Activities Platoon (LEAP), whose members planned social activities for interns within and outside of work. As usual, my extracurricular activity-loving self signed up for LEAP. Our activities would vary from a simple weekday lunch meetup, to bowling on a Friday evening at an arcade, to barbecue and drinks at a fellow intern's residence.

These events were attended by interns in various business units within Lockheed, interns working for other NASA contractors like Jacobs and KBR-Wyle, and interns that worked directly for NASA JSC. These were the perfect no-pressure avenues to network and learn about the different opportunities and varying work types within an aerospace company. With my peers, there was less pressure to seem smart so there were no dumb questions during these conversations.

As an undergraduate aerospace student, I was learning a bit of everything in school— from materials and structures to propulsions and engine design. In the real world, there were engineers and interns working in these diverse aerospace engineering groups, from the development of thermal protective material for Orion to the design of its reaction control thrusters for guidance, navigation, and control. Thus, I could get unfiltered information from fellow interns about what these diverse disciplines entailed and if I was interested in working in a similar area for another internship within or outside Lockheed. These conversations also provided helpful information on pay and compensation for the upper-level students who were getting full-time offers upon graduation. *I mean, you need to know the going rate for somebody with your qualifications. Right?*

~~~~~~~~~~~~~~~~~~~~~~~~~~~~~~~

LEARN TO FLY NUGGET: LEARN FROM FELLOW INTERNS. ASK WHAT THEY ARE WORKING ON AND LISTEN, ACTIVELY. THIS WILL HELP YOU DETERMINE WHAT SOUNDS INTERESTING AND WHAT DOESN'T EXCITE YOU. KNOWING THIS IS HELPFUL FOR A FUTURE INTERNSHIP, FULL-TIME POSITION, OR EVEN TARGETED LEARNING/CLASSES BACK IN SCHOOL.

~~~~~~~~~~~~~~~~~~~~~~~~~~~~~~~

As a LEAP member who planned and attended LEAP events, I also became well acquainted with the HR representative that worked with my intern cohort. She had non-technical oversight into our activities and could provide recommendations during event planning. Sometimes, she even attended our events. As the summer ended, she asked me if I would like to return to the company for another internship, but this time I would work with another team to get different exposure and learning opportunities. She must have also asked for and received feedback from my manager before extending a return offer to me. I was pleased, grateful, and verbally agreed to return. I had learned a lot and would be honored to work once again at a highly sought-after aerospace company.

I ended my internship two weeks earlier than most interns to return to school for intensive three-week residence assistance training. However, I was happy to go back to school with a renewed interest in my aerospace classes as my internship had shown me I had more to learn. I was also tired of the routine full-time commuter grind of waking up early to beat traffic so that I could commute home in time to pack my lunch, shower, and sleep early enough to do it all the next day. School was less routine, and I loved that. I was also going to be in my own space for the first time with a private room and bath; however, I'd have the additional responsibilities of being an RA.

During RA training, I learned how to be a first responder for students, how to resolve conflict between residents, and how to properly document incidents. I would apply these skills to overseeing forty undergraduate students within my direct purview and another four hundred plus students in the hall. The number of people I knew on campus was predicted to increase significantly by virtue of my RA position. Thus, my on-campus life would become a fishbowl visible to many students and staff. Nonetheless, I received a host of professional and life skills that I applied in my role as RA, as SWE president, and simply as me.

However, I had to manage my RA job, SWE president role, and still stay on top of my scholastic endeavors. Even though my plate was full, I was excited to be back at school with my renewed enthusiasm to learn everything aerospace after I had spent time with real aerospace engineers, working on a real spacecraft that would go to the moon.

Taking Flight

Coincidentally, upon my return to school, I took my first class in astronautics. An aerospace degree is truly a fusion of aeronautics and astronautics. The former focuses primarily on everything that flies below the theoretical Karman line located 100km above the Earth's surface, from small unpiloted air vehicles (aka drones) with short battery lives to large passenger-carrying aircraft that fly at high speeds across continents. Astronautics, on the other hand, covers flight that can begin on the surface of the Earth but extends past the Karman line. This includes rocket launches of spacecraft, such as Orion, deployment of small satellites around the Earth, and descent, entry, and landing on Mars.

In astronautics, I was learning the different kind of orbits a spacecraft could have around a large planet; orbits could be circular, elliptical, parabolic, or hyperbolic. I discovered that a spacecraft in an elliptical orbit had a furthest and closest distance to the large planet, called an apoapsis and a periapsis, respectively. I learned how to ·calculate these parameters for various orbits and planets. My mind was blown, considering my recent experiences working on Orion.

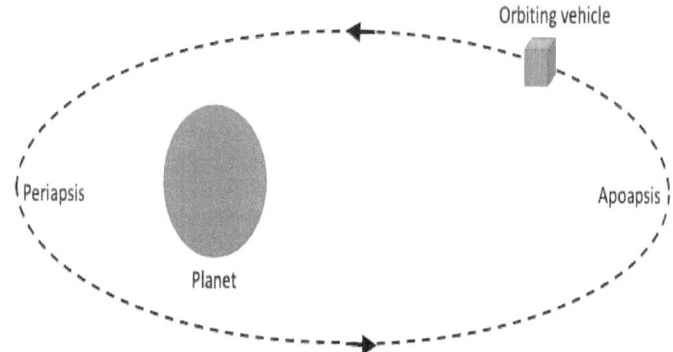

Figure 7: Elliptical orbit of a vehicle around a planet depicting locations of the apoapsis and periapsis.

I also took a class and met a professor that would later change the trajectory of my aerospace career. This class was flight dynamics, and the professor would later become my Ph.D. research advisor.

Before flight dynamics, we had assumed aerospace vehicles were simple objects that could only move in three Cartesian coordinate directions, namely x, y, and z. We hadn't learned how a vehicle in the air, with the same location in x, y, and z could have multiple, vastly different configurations represented by different angles. These angles described how the vehicle was oriented relative to itself, relative to the direction of the wind (angle-of-attack, alpha and sideslip angle, beta), or even relative to a fixed non-moving inertial[19] reference frame (psi, theta, and phi angles).

In addition to numbers and letters of the English alphabet, my notebook was now full of these angles represented by alpha, beta, psi, theta, and phi. At some point I told my classmate, "This all sounds like Greek," pointing to a theta in my notes. She replied, "Literally," and we had a good laugh.

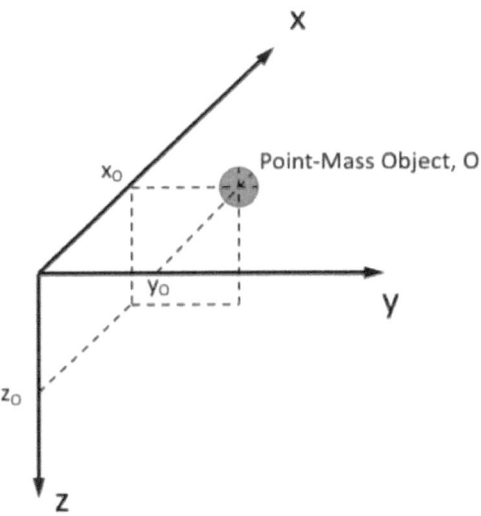

Figure 8: Point-Mass Object, O located at point x_0, y_0, z_0 in Cartesian Coordinate Frame xyz

---

[19] An inertial frame is a non-accelerating reference frame. It could be a moving frame but if its speed is constant, it can be considered an inertial frame.

I was also learning that we could define a coordinate frame on an aircraft in which the x-direction points out of the aircraft's nose (where the pilot sits), the y-direction points out towards the right wing, and the z-direction points down towards the ground. This forms a right-handed coordinate system so if you point the four fingers of your right hand (excluding the thumb) in the direction of x, and you curl them towards y, your thumb should always point in the direction of z. *Use Figure 9 as a guide and try it!*

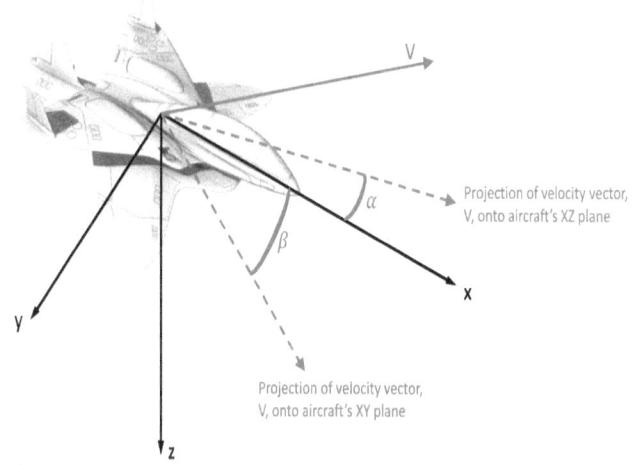

Figure 9: Aircraft drawing showing coordinate frame, angle of attack, α, and sideslip, β.

Although flight dynamics was interesting, it was complex. There were concepts I didn't understand when they were introduced, and I would sometimes refrain from asking questions during the class. Instead, I noted questions at the top margin of each page, and after class, I would go to my professor and ask them all.

Most times, all I needed was a quick verbal clarification from him. Other times, we would both write and draw on a corner of the whiteboard as he helped me clear up my confusion.

I had previously learned to use my notebook margins in high school when I was fortuitously placed next to a diligent student who noted key points for each page in her book's page margins. I marveled at how she condensed large amounts of information into a few concise sentences and modified her technique to include questions on my page briefs—questions I could ask other classmates or professors after the class.

~~~~~~~~~~~~~~~~~~~~~~~~~~~~~~~~~

LEARN TO FLY NUGGET: IF YOU DON'T WANT TO ASK IN CLASS, WRITE DOWN KEY CONCEPTS/REMINDERS AND ANY QUESTIONS AT THE TOP OF YOUR

NOTEBOOK PAGE AND ASK STUDENTS OR PROFESSORS TO EXPLAIN AFTER THE CLASS.

~~~~~~~~~~~~~~~~~~~~~~~~~~~~~~~~~~

In the fall, I also took a class called Incompressible Aerodynamics or simply Incompressibles, which covered the dynamics of fluids (gases and liquids) that move slowly. Slow in this class was defined as anything slower than the speed of sound at a specific temperature, also referred to as Mach 1.[20]

Incompressibles covered a significant amount of material, and I struggled to keep up with the lightening pace of the instructor. After looking for the content he taught and not finding it in the required textbook, I asked him if he could recommend additional reading material that could improve my comprehension. He recommended two textbooks, and one of them saved me. I checked every library I had an affiliation with and succeeding in finding it at my best friend's university in Houston. She borrowed it for me, and I proceeded to add it to my Incompressibles study material. At the end of the semester, I heard two students got an

---

[20] The Mach number is the ratio of an object's speed to the speed of sound at the same temperature.

A in Incompressibles: me and another, out of about twenty students.

~~~~~~~~~~~~~~~~~~~~~~~~~~~~~~~~

LEARN TO FLY NUGGET: IF YOUR REQUIRED TEXTBOOK ISN'T HELPING, (1) CHECK YOUR SYLLABUS FOR RECOMMENDED TEXTBOOKS, OR (2) ASK YOUR PROFESSOR FOR RECOMMENDED TEXTBOOKS. YOU CAN GET OLDER EDITIONS FROM YOUR LIBRARY OR OTHER UNIVERSITY LIBRARIES THROUGH A FRIEND OR INTERLIBRARY LOAN.

~~~~~~~~~~~~~~~~~~~~~~~~~~~~~~~~

Turbulence

During the spring of the same school year, I got my first truly deserved B grade, and it broke my heart. It was with the most unassuming friendly teacher, whom I got along well-enough with, in a course called Compressible Flow.

In this class, we learned how to accelerate or decelerate gases flowing through a tube by changing the size of the tube. We also learned about shock waves and how they form at high speeds and change the properties of surrounding air. Compressible fluid flow was straightforward, and I was on a path to an A. I did every homework problem, aced midterms and even the final exam, but then the last few weeks of the class something happened.

We all had to complete a final project that required us to write a computer program that would numerically solve a problem. Let me describe what a numerical solver is: Assume you don't know that 2 + 5 = 7, and you're required to figure out what number you must add to 2 to get 7. A numerical solver iteratively adds a number to 2, compares the answer to your desired 7, and continues adding a number until its answer and your desired 7 are close enough.

If the solver finds that difference between its answer and your desired 7 is tiny, say 0.00001, the numeric solver chooses the number that produced that tiny difference as your answer. When that happens, your code is said to have converged to a solution. This is a very simple loop you can write using any simple programming language of your choice such as C, MATLAB, or Python.

I had taken an introductory programming class before Compressible Flow, however I (and likely many others), simply did what we were asked to do in the programming class and didn't quite learn how to independently write a program for our own objectives.

So, I wrote my crappy code for the Compressible Flow project, and it didn't converge to a solution. To pass the project, which was 5% of our final grade, my code simply had to converge to a solution. To get the full 5%, my code had to converge to the correct solution. I heard that only one student got the 5% by getting his code to converge to the right solution. Another student's code converged but wasn't quite right, so he got a 3%. The rest of us scored anywhere between 0% and 2% and were promptly assigned "Incomplete" as our overall final grade till we submitted a code that converged. After submission of a converged working code, our letter grade would be changed from "Incomplete". However, our final grade was still based on our first project score. Thus, if you got a 0% on your first project submission and a 5% on your second attempt, your cumulative final grade was still determined using the 0%. *Tough love.*

It was unfortunate because I was on the trajectory to land at an A and a project worth only 5% derailed that. Prior to the project, my cumulative grade in the class was likely around 87% out of 95%, and getting an additional 3% on the project would have given me an A. Getting 0% on the other hand was a loss that led to a B.

I was used to being one of the top students that somehow won in the end, but this time, I didn't. However, I had to give myself some grace because I had extracurricular activities including being a resident assistant that sometimes required me to be on call at nighttime, being the SWE president that led meetings and oversaw the effective running of the organization, and being on the dance team for the African Students organization with dance practice multiple times a week and performing on and off campus. I was swamped and that B was inevitable.

~~~~~~~~~~~~~~~~~~~~~~~~~~~~~~~~

LEARN TO FLY NUGGET: LEARN HOW TO WRITE SIMPLE PROGRAMS IF YOU ARE IN AN ENGINEERING FIELD. THERE ARE FREE CLASSES ON YOUTUBE, MIT OPENCOURSEWARE, COURSE ERA, UDACITY, STANFORD, AND OTHER UNIVERSITIES. JUST DO A GOOGLE SEARCH FOR FREE PROGRAMMING CLASSES.

~~~~~~~~~~~~~~~~~~~~~~~~~~~~~~~~

Little Things Make A Huge Difference

I lost my 4.0 that semester and became insouciant about getting all As. I felt like there was no difference between a 3.95 and 3.2 GPA: They both start with 3 so who cares? Well apparently, the world cares and graduating honors distinctions (cum laude, magna cum laude, and summa cum laude) are dependent on the GPA range between 3 and 4. Even though I had permanently lost my perfect 4.0 that semester, I still received the award for Highest Honors in the Honors College where I had two scholarships.

In addition, I received an unexpected scholarship from the College of Engineering (COE) based solely on my scholastic achievements—no application required. The fortuitous scholarship notification letter came from the COE Dean for Student Affairs, and I immediately typed a thank you letter to her outlining my gratitude and plans for the scholarship money. I slid the signed thank you letter under her office door and didn't think anything else of it.

Exactly one year later, right around graduation, this same Dean said to me, in the presence of other students, that of all the students that were awarded those scholarships, only one of them contacted her to say thank you. That student was me. A fellow classmate who heard this smirked and called me a goody-two-shoes but that didn't faze me in the least. I was thankful and do not regret showing my appreciation.

~~~~~~~~~~~~~~~~~~~~~~~~~~~~~

LEARN TO FLY NUGGET: IN ALL THINGS, GIVE THANKS. SAY THANK YOU FOR THE LITTLE THINGS AND THE BIG THINGS. BE KIND & POLITE TO THE JANITOR AND TO THE UNIVERSITY PRESIDENT. GRACE AND GOOD MANNERS WILL TAKE YOU FAR.

~~~~~~~~~~~~~~~~~~~~~~~~~~~~~

As the SWE president, I oversaw the effective running of the organization and this included but was not limited to serving as the ultimate representative and spokesperson within and outside the organization, presiding over all board and general body meetings, ensuring spending was in line with annual budgets, and liaising with our university advisor and the external SWE organization—national and regional bodies included. In addition, it was also my responsibility to identify and preclude any inefficiencies or challenges that prevented the organization's success in any way.

When I assumed the position, I discovered that there were several tasks that previous president(s) had carried out that should have been completed by the other elected officers. It was likely easier for the initiator of this approach to do it all. However, this was inefficient and made the transition to a new board difficult. *How would a new treasurer understand her role if the outgoing treasurer deferred to the president on most financial matters?* In addition, I also noticed the outgoing board was composed primarily of upper-level students, primarily seniors. Thus, after their graduation, the expertise of running a student organization left with them.

To tackle these challenges, I instituted a few changes. First, I created a Freshman Recruitment (FR) position. The FR officer would recruit freshmen into the organization by distributing SWE promotional material outside freshmen STEM classes and speaking to the students for a few minutes, with permission of the professors. Through this approach, we were able to increase freshmen participation in the organization by a whooping 40%! We had freshmen involvement on the board and increased freshman attendance in our general body meetings.

When I did the math and quantified the increase, I was stoked and promptly updated my resume with this information. The description of my role as president went from this:

> *President - Society of Women Engineers, UTA*
> *Fall 2008 – Spring 2009*
> *Oversee the effective running of the organization, serve as the organization spokesperson within and outside the university, and preside over all meetings.*

To this:

> *President - Society of Women Engineers, UTA*
> *Fall 2008 – Spring 2009*
> - *Increased freshman participation in organization by **40%** by instituting a freshman retention officer position.*
> - *Streamlined processes and enhanced organization's effectiveness by proper delegation and tailoring of officer roles and responsibilities.*

There's nothing wrong with the first description. However, there's nothing remarkable about it either. Everyone knows the role of a president, but everyone doesn't know what I did as the president. My resume is my opportunity to tell them.

~~~~~~~~~~~~~~~~~~~~~~~~~~~~~~~~~~~

LEARN TO FLY NUGGET: ON YOUR RESUME, QUANTIFY YOUR CONTRIBUTIONS AND ACHIEVEMENTS IN SCHOLASTIC AND EXTRACURRICULAR ACTIVITIES. THINK CAREFULLY ABOUT PROCESS IMPROVEMENTS YOU HAVE MADE AND GIVE YOURSELF THE CREDIT YOU DESERVE.

~~~~~~~~~~~~~~~~~~~~~~~~~~~~~~~~~~~

On the second challenge of too many tasks falling on the president, I made it my duty to ensure that each officer carried out their roles as described in the by-laws. I felt that this would (A) facilitate a smooth transition to the next set of officers for the next academic year, and (B) prevent me and future presidents burning out from too much SWE work. However, this was a non-trivial challenge, as I realized one day.

Our organization needed to conduct some financial business with the university bursar. As the president, I signed the required form, placed it on a desk in the SWE office, and told the treasurer to take the form to the bursar and do what was needed.

She picked up the form and went to the building across the campus, which houses the bursar and other administrative offices, but couldn't complete the task. Perhaps there was a queue and she had to leave for a class or even commute back home. All I know is that she brought the form back to the office with a curt note for me to do it myself.

When I returned to the SWE office, I saw the incomplete form and note and sent her a text along the lines of, "Hi Sue, I just saw the financial form back in our office. Were you unable to go to the bursar?" Immediately, she sent back the most dramatic angry response, "You are the worst president ever! Our previous president was never this bad. I don't want to be treasurer anymore. I quit!"

I was shocked but also hurt. I didn't know where this anger was coming from, and I didn't know how to respond so I didn't. Instead, I marched to the sixth floor of our building, to our SWE advisor's office, phone in hand, ready to read the text and explain the situation. I needed to know something wasn't wrong with me. *It was her, right? It had to be her!*

I stood in the doorway of our advisor's office and regurgitated everything. Dr. T. listened with such poise and a wry smile that I wondered if I was missing something. I asked her if I did something wrong to which she replied, "No." She explained that nothing was wrong with me, but nothing was wrong with the treasurer either.

"You simply have different communication styles," she said. *Communication? Huh? What sort of variation in communication could warrant such a vicious response?* Dr. T broke it down even further. She said that people like me see an important task and ask, "Hi fellow board officer, can you go to the bursar and handle this financial issue by tomorrow?" Moving quickly, and disregarding pleasantries, we are task-oriented and forget to connect with the people of whom we are making these requests. Our treasurer would have benefited from a more people-oriented request along the lines of "Hi fellow board officer, our organization needs this financial issue handled as soon as possible. Do you have time in your schedule today or tomorrow to do this for us?"

With the realization dawning that I may have come across as giving orders to my board officers, I began to appreciate what Dr. T was saying. Sheepishly, I asked, "Will you speak with her also? And what will you tell her?"

"Of course!" She replied, "I will give her the other half of the conversation I just gave you."

The following day, I received an extensive apology from the treasurer via text and a promise to return to the bursar. I couldn't believe it. I also apologized and wondered about the other half of the conversation she had with Dr. T. I wished I could have been a fly on the wall to witness the other half of the magic.

This incident is one of my earliest lessons in leadership and working with others—seeking help when I was helpless and learning that something as seemingly trivial as communication styles could cause conflict and weaken an organization.

~~~~~~~~~~~~~~~~~~~~~~~~~~~~~~~~~

LEARN TO FLY NUGGET: YOU'RE NEVER REALLY ALONE AND CAN ALWAYS ASK FOR HELP. THERE ARE EXPERIENCED PEOPLE ALL AROUND WHO EITHER GET PAID TO HELP YOU OR ARE HAPPY TO HELP YOU BASED ON THEIR OWN EXPERIENCES AND WISDOM. SEEK HELP WHENEVER YOU ARE STUCK, CONFUSED, OR OVERWHELMED.

~~~~~~~~~~~~~~~~~~~~~~~~~~~~~~~~~

Find Your Niche

That year, I attended the SWE national conference once again. I had already secured a return internship offer after my first internship with Lockheed Martin, so I didn't have the pressure to network with the large aerospace company representatives present. Instead, I was driven by genuine curiosity during the career fair.

I visited the booths at the periphery of the exhibit hall where the smaller aerospace companies, who were typically contractors for the larger companies, were located. Academic institutions such as universities, university-affiliated research laboratories, government research laboratories, and engineering organizations such as the American Society for Engineering Education (ASEE) were also present on the fringes at the exhibit hall.

I stopped by the Stanford University booth and met a graduate school recruitment representative whom I talked to. I was a first semester junior at the time and hadn't quite considered going to graduate school. I figured I would get my "dream job" likely at Lockheed Martin, work for a few years, then get my master's degree while working full time. That was the route I saw more commonly with engineers I considered successful, some of whom I met during my first internship.

I entertained the conversation with the graduate school recruiter while wondering why a university, especially one as renowned as Stanford, would send a representative to recruit students to its graduate school programs. I would later come to understand when I got into the world of research during my senior year that recruiting top students was important for EVERY university. The recruiter and I exchanged contact information and at his urging, I promised to consider Stanford University's engineering programs for graduate school.

~~~~~~~~~~~~~~~~~~~~~~~~~~~~~

LEARN TO FLY NUGGET: DON'T FORGET THE LESS POPULAR BOOTHS AT CAREER FAIRS SUCH AS UNIVERSITIES AND SMALL COMPANIES. UNIVERSITY RECRUITERS WILL SHARE FUNDING AVAILABLE TO NEW STUDENTS SO YOU CAN GO TO SCHOOL FOR FREE OR AT A REDUCED COST. SMALLER COMPANIES MAY ALSO BE MORE WILLING TO OFFER YOU AN INTERNSHIP OR JOB OFFER IF THE BIG ONES DON'T.

~~~~~~~~~~~~~~~~~~~~~~~~~~~~~

As I casually explored the less popular booths, I stumbled on the CIA booth. *The United States Central Intelligence Agency was also recruiting at the National Conference of the Society of Women Engineers? Wait, what? Why?* I took myself there fast! I couldn't even hide my shock and awe from the first representative I met. She was a young mathematician who worked for the CIA. I promptly asked her what an aerospace engineer could do at the CIA and showed her my resume. She didn't say much but referred me to a soft-spoken, short-haired, black female boss whom I immediately "fan-girled" over.

The CIA boss perused my resume and told me I looked like I would be a great fit for the agency. I asked again, "What could you do with an aerospace engineer?" She replied that the CIA may not use the aerospace engineering degree per se. However, the critical and analytical problem-solving skills you gain with a STEM degree are invaluable to an agency like the CIA.

The ability to recognize patterns, identify relevant features, diagnose, and prognosticate over diverse or niche scenarios are skills utilized in maintaining national safety and security. We exchanged contact information and she promised to call me to extend a verbal tentative offer for an internship.

After the conference, the CIA boss called me to provide additional details about the kinds of things I could do during my internship at the CIA. I would have to move to DC for the summer and from what I gathered the pay was not competitive. She also couldn't provide a formal written offer without a tentative acceptance from me. Her offer was that I would be performing a service to the country and performing potentially impactful work.

I appreciated her honesty in letting me know that I wouldn't make a lot of money working for the CIA. I was disappointed because I was intrigued at the thought of working for the CIA, but I knew that not only would I make less than I would at Lockheed Martin, but I would also spend more on living expenses in the Washington, DC area. If I went back to Lockheed Martin, I would make more and I wouldn't have to pay rent as I would live with my sister, who had moved even closer to the Bay Area, Houston. So, I said no to the CIA and went back to Lockheed Martin.

This time, I worked with Orion's Hatch Mechanisms team within the Mechanical Engineering division. Using ProE, a professional engineering AutoCAD design software, I spent most of my internship designing test fixtures for Orion hatches.[21] These designs would later be used for testing and verification to ensure that the hatches could withstand vibration and thermal stresses[22] associated with spacecraft entry and reentry. My second internship was a great experience and once again, showed me how little I knew. I returned to school for my final academic year with the best laid plans: to get an offer from Lockheed Martin in the fall, graduate in the spring of the following year, and start a full-time position as an aerospace engineer. I had no idea how that final year would change everything.

---

[21] "A hatch is an opening with an operable, sealable cover that ensures the isolation of adjoining environments and allows passage of people and cargo/equipment from one environment to the other." Ref: NASA (https://www.nasa.gov/sites/default/files/atoms/files/vehicle_hatches_technical_brief_ochmo.pdf)

[22] During reentry, spacecraft are subjected to high temperatures, vibrations, and acoustic loads that they must withstand to keep the spacecraft, crew, and payload safe.

LEARN TO FLY NUGGETS

GIVE A FIRM HANDSHAKE AND LOOK
PEOPLE IN THE EYE WHEN YOU ARE
INTRODUCED. NOTE ANY IDENTIFYING
CHARACTERISTICS WITH THE NAMES
AFTER YOU MEET THEM SO YOU CAN
REMEMBER THEIR NAMES. USE THEIR
NAMES IN CONVERSATION WITH THEM.
BE PRESENT.

TAKE NOTES DURING MEETINGS TO
KEEP YOURSELF ALERT. IF POSSIBLE, EAT
LUNCH OUTSIDE AND/OR TAKE QUICK
WALKS OUTSIDE IN THE FRESH AIR TO
BREAK UP YOUR DAY. CAFFEINE ALSO
HELPS. IF YOU FALL ASLEEP DURING A
MEETING, GIVE YOURSELF SOME GRACE.
IT'S OK.

LEARN FROM FELLOW INTERNS. ASK
WHAT THEY ARE WORKING ON AND
LISTEN ACTIVELY. THIS WILL HELP YOU
DETERMINE WHAT SOUNDS
INTERESTING AND WHAT DOESN'T
EXCITE YOU. KNOWING THIS IS HELPFUL
FOR A FUTURE INTERNSHIP, FULL-TIME

POSITION, OR EVEN TARGETED
LEARNING/CLASSES BACK IN SCHOOL.
IF YOU DON'T WANT TO ASK IN CLASS,
WRITE DOWN KEY
CONCEPTS/REMINDERS AND ANY
QUESTIONS AT THE TOP OF YOUR
NOTEBOOK PAGE AND ASK STUDENTS
OR PROFESSORS TO EXPLAIN AFTER THE
CLASS.

IF YOUR REQUIRED TEXTBOOK ISN'T
HELPING, (1) CHECK YOUR SYLLABUS FOR
RECOMMENDED TEXTBOOKS, OR (2) ASK
YOUR PROFESSOR FOR RECOMMENDED
TEXTBOOKS. YOU CAN GET OLDER
EDITIONS FROM YOUR LIBRARY OR
OTHER UNIVERSITY LIBRARIES THROUGH
A FRIEND OR INTERLIBRARY LOAN.

LEARN HOW TO WRITE SIMPLE
PROGRAMS IF YOU ARE IN AN
ENGINEERING FIELD. THERE ARE FREE
CLASSES ON YOUTUBE, MIT
OPENCOURSEWARE, COURSE ERA,
UDACITY, STANFORD, AND OTHER
UNIVERSITIES. JUST DO A GOOGLE

SEARCH FOR FREE PROGRAMMING CLASSES.

IN ALL THINGS, GIVE THANKS. SAY THANK YOU FOR THE LITTLE THINGS AND THE BIG THINGS. BE KIND AND POLITE TO THE JANITOR AND TO THE UNIVERSITY PRESIDENT. GRACE AND GOOD MANNERS WILL TAKE YOU FAR.

ON YOUR RESUME, QUANTIFY YOUR CONTRIBUTIONS AND ACHIEVEMENTS IN SCHOLASTIC AND EXTRACURRICULAR ACTIVITIES. THINK CAREFULLY ABOUT PROCESS IMPROVEMENTS YOU HAVE MADE AND GIVE YOURSELF THE CREDIT YOU DESERVE.

YOU'RE NEVER REALLY ALONE AND CAN ALWAYS ASK FOR HELP. THERE ARE EXPERIENCED PEOPLE ALL AROUND WHO EITHER GET PAID TO HELP YOU OR ARE HAPPY TO HELP YOU BASED ON THEIR OWN EXPERIENCES AND WISDOM. SEEK HELP WHENEVER YOU ARE STUCK, CONFUSED, OR OVERWHELMED.

DON'T FORGET THE LESS POPULAR
BOOTHS AT CAREER FAIRS SUCH AS
UNIVERSITIES AND SMALL COMPANIES.
UNIVERSITY RECRUITERS WILL SHARE
FUNDING AVAILABLE TO NEW STUDENTS
SO YOU CAN GO TO SCHOOL FOR FREE
OR AT A REDUCED COST. SMALLER
COMPANIES MAY ALSO BE MORE WILLING
TO OFFER YOU AN INTERNSHIP OR JOB
OFFER IF THE BIG ONES DON'T.

Senior Year (Year Four)

Changing Gears

In the fall of 2009, after my second internship at Lockheed Martin, President Obama's administration initiated a substantial downsizing of the U.S. government's space program and began to outsource huge swaths of the space program to the private aerospace sector and space travel startups. A review committee deemed the schedule for the Constellation program, which included Orion, unrealistic without a significant increase in budget.[23]

This committee recommended that Constellation be canceled in favor of research to reduce the cost of crewed spaceflight. Their recommendations also included support for commercial flights to the international space station. The committee's suggestions, which were heeded, drastically changed the NASA human exploration and space technology portfolio, along with the

---

[23] Source: Encyclopedia Brittanica, "Constellation Program": https://www.britannica.com/science/Constellation-program

established aerospace companies that contracted with NASA to support this portfolio.

Lockheed Martin was one of those companies. The students with whom I had interned the previous summer, who were a year ahead of me in school and had already received full-time employment offers, swiftly had them retracted. Although Orion remained and resurfaced under a different program, the situation was too uncertain for these companies to hire new employees when work was rumored to be going away. I still had a full academic year to find a job, so I wasn't worried. I figured I would use the time to explore other options, so I started to put feelers out.

That same fall, I stumbled upon a new program my school offered called the MavGrad Engineering program. It was a program that allowed high-achieving undergraduate students to skip a master's degree and go straight to a Doctor of Philosophy degree (Ph.D.). I wasn't even considering graduate studies (master's or Ph.D.) before I found this program. I knew a little about a master's degree but not too much about a Ph.D. However, Dr. Wendy A. Okolo had a nice ring to it. Furthermore, although I had enjoyed my internship experiences, they showed me that there was still a lot I had to learn in school. I also wasn't quite ready to grow up and figured that graduate school would provide a brief reprieve from adulting, commuting, and waking up early.

I attended an information session about this B.S. to Ph.D. program and learned that unlike an undergraduate degree, most STEM Ph.D. programs were fully funded, and Ph.D. students didn't have to pay their tuition out of pocket. Universities would cover tuition and fees for the student and provide financial support in the form of monthly stipends in exchange for the student working as a professor's teaching assistant (TA).

As a TA, I would work closely with a professor to create and grade homework problems and projects, administer and proctor exams, manage online course material and student records, hold office hours to provide additional tutoring help, and sometimes even teach the class in the professor's stead. There were also external fellowships[24] that provided the stipend and paid all tuition and fees with no TA requirement. Financially, this was a great deal if I didn't compare it to the real world where I would be making more than double the salary of a Ph.D. student.

---

[24] Fellowships are like scholarships in that they provide financial support to students, however they are for graduate students and don't have teaching assistantship requirements. This enables the recipients to focus solely on their own coursework and research.

However, to successfully complete a Ph.D., a student must first choose a field of research, understand the state of the art of that field, conduct research in the field, with the guidance of a research advisor (a.k.a., dissertation advisor), and most importantly, make an original contribution to the chosen field. *Gosh!*

I didn't understand what it meant to do research, but I knew that the people that did it didn't have two heads. I could do it too. I also learned that I may need the Graduate Records Examinations (GRE) that would test how well I could write, how critically I could think, and how adequately I could reason, both verbally and quantitatively. This sounded like the SAT I had taken at 15. I was now 20 and figured I could handle a more rigorous scholastic test. Depending on the school or graduate program, the GRE is not always required and can be considered by some to be a trivial graduate school admissions formality. I wasn't required to take it at my university, as I had good grades and had established a track record of success. However, I decided to take it anyway, just in case.

The GRE would later prove important for me almost two years later when I applied and successfully received over $100,000 to fund my Ph.D. under the National Defense Science and Engineering Graduate (NDSEG) fellowship.

~~~~~~~~~~~~~~~~~~~~~~~~~~~~~~~~~

**LEARN TO FLY NUGGET: JUST BECAUSE
IT'S NOT REQUIRED DOESN'T MEAN
YOU SHOULD SKIP IT. UNDERSTAND
AND WEIGH THE FUTURE BENEFITS
OF A SEEMINGLY UNNECESSARY
HURDLE.**

~~~~~~~~~~~~~~~~~~~~~~~~~~~~~~~~~

Saying Yes

While I was understanding the pros and cons of graduate school and research, I was still taking the penultimate set of my undergraduate courses. I was enrolled in an introductory Automatic Controls class, taught by the same professor who taught us flight dynamics the previous school year. In Automatic Controls we learned how to understand dynamic systems and use our understanding to design controllers that would move the system from one state to another. By knowing how a system works, having an idea of where that system is, and knowing where you want the system to be, control theory and design gives you the tools to move the system to where you want it.

Simplistically, consider driving your old Toyota Rav4 (known system) at 60 miles per hour (idea of system speed) down the highway and needing to increase the speed to 75 miles per hour (where you want the system to be): You know exactly how much pressure to apply to the gas pedal to increase your speed at a rate that is acceptable to you. That seemingly intuitive knowledge is the crux of controls design. *How well do you know your system? How accurate are the sensors that are telling you about the state of your system? Is your desired state achievable? Is it achievable in the timeframe you would like? Are there external factors to consider that could prevent you from reaching your desired state?* There were many questions and performance requirements to consider in the design of a controller.

Just like the flight dynamics class, this class was one of my favorites and one day after class, our professor took a few minutes to share something with us.

When a bird flies, it creates a nonuniform airflow behind it. As a result, another bird flying in certain regions of the nonuniform airflow requires less energy to fly. The energy-saving regions for the trailing bird are behind and to the right or left of the leading bird. In fact, nature has shown that birds fly in a V-formation when flying long distances, such as

Canada geese migrating south in the winter.[25] This configuration reduces the aerodynamic drag[26] force experienced by each trailing bird due to the wing-tip vortices and nonuniform airflow generated by the preceding birds. These intelligent birds intuitively know exactly where to position themselves in the formation to experience less drag, conserve energy, and thus, fly longer.

Figure 10: Migrating birds flying in a V formation[27].

---

[25] https://www.nationalgeographic.com/animals/article/do-canada-geese-still-fly-south-for-winter

[26] Drag is a force that acts to impede motion and slow an object. Caused by friction and air pressure differences, drag acts in the opposite direction of an object's motion.

[27] https://pixabay.com/photos/migratory-birds-cranes-4027722/

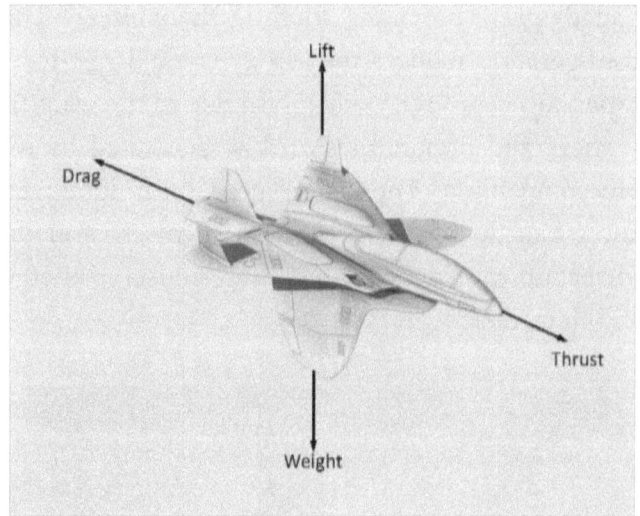

Figure 11: Aircraft showing the lift, weight, thrust, and drag forces.

Based on this phenomenal improvement in aerodynamic performance for birds, researchers are now studying how aircraft can fly in formation and obtain similar benefits. A reduction in drag for a plane directly translates to a decrease in the thrust[28] force that the plane's engines must generate. This has significant financial impact, as a decrease in thrust leads to a corresponding reduction in aviation fuel. For context, in 2017, U.S. airlines consumed approximately 17.3 billion gallons of fuel at $1.69 a

---

[28] Thrust propels a vehicle forward in the direction of motion. Created with a propeller, jet engine, or rocket, thrust is the force that drag opposes.

gallon.[29] Fuel savings of even one percent translate to savings of almost 300 million dollars!

In addition, the different aircraft in the formation don't need to begin or end their flights from the same takeoff or landing locations, respectively, to realize these benefits. They could fly in formation wherever their different flight trajectories align. For instance, planes leaving different parts of the continental U.S. for Europe or Africa will have flight trajectories that align over the Atlantic. Those planes could benefit from formation flight over the regions where their flight paths align.

The U.S. Air Force Research Laboratory (AFRL) was interested in the potential of this aircraft formation flight research as applied to military aircraft flight. Our controls professor was accepted to the U.S. Air Force (USAF) Summer Faculty Fellowship Program (USAF-SFFP) to conduct research on aircraft formation flight at the AFRL the following summer. Beginning the following year, USAF-SFFP professors were allowed to bring one graduate student with them. The eligibility requirements for the graduate student included U.S. citizenship and enrollment in graduate school the

---

[29] https://www.nationalgeographic.com/environment/urban-expeditions/transportation/green-aviation1/

semester following the summer fellowship program.[30]

As our professor presented the research and potential opportunity, my interest in the work, and in graduate school, increased. I fervently hoped he would choose me for this wonderful opportunity. I met all the eligibility requirements to accompany him to the AFRL location at the Wright-Patterson Air Force Base in Ohio. I was excited that I would get paid a pretty stipend to work with brilliant researchers at an Air Force Base and ultimately get a Ph.D. *Was this even real life?*

I rushed to him after class, "Yes sir, please, I would like to apply for the position. Do you need anything like a resume or transcript? Please just let me know." He asked if I would go to graduate school after finishing my undergraduate degree in seven months and I responded with a resounding yes. That was all he needed. I didn't realize it, but I had already established a positive reputation before him, as I had scored an A in his Flight Dynamics course and still now worked diligently to understand the material in his Automatic Controls class, listening with rapt attention to everything he said. As in the previous course, I would ask additional questions after class

---

[30] http://afsffp.sysplus.com/SFFP/about/eligibility.aspx

and even take a piece of chalk to the board to work with him and demystify the course content.

He chose me and collected my information to provide to the administrators of the USAF-SFFP. The plan was that the following semester, for a few hours each week, he would familiarize me with the project and research tools for the aircraft formation flight work. That would be my introduction to the nebulous but seemingly prestigious thing called research. I would work closely with him while I rounded out my course work for my bachelor's degree.

That same fall semester, I took an aerospace Senior Design course. It was the first in a series of two capstone courses required to graduate as an aerospace engineer. This class was set up to cover the complete design and analysis of a full aerospace system. It included the technical construct, market analysis, configuration design, mission specification, and the integration of the varying aerospace engineering disciplines such as controls, propulsions, structures, aerodynamics, and systems engineering. We would spend the full academic year, i.e., fall and spring semesters, on the complete but conceptual design of an aerospace vehicle.

Senior Design was abstract and the metrics to determine pass or fail were not as clearly defined as my previous courses. The course was structured to teach us how to perform in the real world and work with a multi-disciplinary team to develop, share, and analyze relevant data that would be used to design a conceptual aircraft.

In the real world, pass and fail weren't as binary as a simple cut off mark. In the real world, the suitability of a solution transcends pass or fail. Obviously, an aircraft that doesn't fly is an absolute failure in the real world, but an aircraft that has better range or endurance than another is still a perfectly functioning air vehicle. Similarly, a drone with 45-minute battery life may be more acceptable at a certain price point as opposed to one with a 2-hour battery life.

I believe this is what the class attempted to teach us, the subjectivity of design and the realism of real aerospace engineering work. However, since the class and project goals were so multidisciplinary, the grading scheme was tenuous. Your work as a discipline lead is dependent on the other disciplines and vice versa, so how exactly does an impartial grader determine which team member gets an A grade and which team member from the same team gets a B grade? Although the definition of success was vague, I enjoyed the class as our professor taught us about aerospace vehicle design with his numerous real-world stories and examples.

He taught us about the design of the fastest jet in the world, the Lockheed SR-71 Blackbird. I discovered how instrumental the innovative aerospace engineer, Clarence "Kelly" Johnson, was in the vehicle's design. Kelly Johnson sounded like the Steve Jobs of the aircraft design world. For us young impressionable aerospace students, such a status sounded like a fantasy, only something we aspired to and dreamed of.

I had never even heard of the SR-71 or Kelly Johnson before Senior Design. Some of the students had heard of Kelly though. Others only knew about the SR-71 Blackbird. Some students were familiar with both Kelly Johnson and the SR-71 Blackbird, and they nodded knowingly and chimed in whenever he discussed aerospace history. We were a diverse group that included aircraft pilots, aviation history buffs, and students whose parents were in the aerospace industry. I was none of that. Still, I chugged on.

Figure 12: Me in my senior design class

~~~~~~~~~~~~~~~~~~~~~~~~~~~~~~~~

LEARN TO FLY NUGGET: YOU WILL BE IN ROOMS WITH PEOPLE THAT HAVE MORE EXPERIENCE AND SEEM TO KNOW SO MUCH MORE. THAT'S ALRIGHT BECAUSE EVERYTHING IS FOR EVERYONE. ALWAYS GO BACK TO WHAT YOU KNOW. DUE DILIGENCE WILL TAKE YOU FAR.

~~~~~~~~~~~~~~~~~~~~~~~~~~~~~~~~

Making a Decision

About halfway through the semester, the professor, with whom many of us were enamored, provided an opportunity to do research with him. Again, this research thing I didn't know about before my final year was now popping up everywhere I looked or didn't look. Senior Design was a fascinating class and several of us expressed interest. He accepted his top students to do research with him and that same semester, we the chosen undergraduate students began conducting multidisciplinary aircraft design research under his tutelage.

We had weekly round table meetings with him where we individually provided updates on what we had achieved the previous week. During these meetings, we also received guidance from him and the graduate student mentors with whom he had paired us.

My task was to create a database in Microsoft Excel of every known unmanned air vehicle (UAV) and classify them by weight, size, range, endurance, purpose, and other specifications. This was research. There was no solution or existing avenue from which I could duplicate the database. I would use several resources such as the internet, history books, or other relevant texts in the engineering library and construct this database. My fellow student researchers had other responsibilities that would fill varying vehicle design needs such as determining engine requirements for an aircraft or developing necessary aerodynamic data for controls design.

Not long after we started the conceptual vehicle design research, I heard about something called the Dean's Undergraduate Research Assistantship (DURA) award. This award provides a small stipend for one semester to enable an undergraduate student to conduct research under a professor. A student could use the money to pay for supplies, procure reference material to conduct a literature review, or even to purchase software such as Microsoft Office suite or even programming software that may be necessary for the research. *Free money again? Sign me up.*

~~~~~~~~~~~~~~~~~~~~~~~~~~~~~~~~~

LEARN TO FLY NUGGET: DO RESEARCH, FOR AT LEAST ONE SEMESTER. ASK THE PROFESSOR OF YOUR FAVORITE CLASS IF YOU CAN DO RESEARCH WITH HER. UNDERGRADUATE RESEARCH EXPERIENCE WILL MAKE YOU

COMPETITIVE FOR THE BEST GRADUATE PROGRAMS, JUST IN CASE YOU CONSIDER GOING TO GRADUATE SCHOOL IN THE FUTURE.

~~~~~~~~~~~~~~~~~~~~~~~~~~~~~~~~~~~

At least three of us applied for the DURA award, which required endorsements from the advising research professor as the final step in the application. I turned in the two applications to the two professors I was conducting research with: the conceptual vehicle design professor and the controls design professor. I got the DURA award under the controls design professor and didn't think much of the other application. I would later find out from another student who submitted a DURA application for conceptual design research that she didn't get it either. *Oh well.*

I had one-on-one weekly meetings with my controls professor to prepare for the summer research we would conduct at the AFRL. On my laptop, I had installed MATLAB and Simulink, a modeling and simulation software for dynamic systems such as ground vehicles, aircraft, and spacecraft. He provided the aircraft formation flight simulation and patiently walked me through every step required to run the simulation, generate results, and analyze the results. I was still a full-time undergraduate student and couldn't do much outside of our time together. This is common with undergraduate student researchers: They can barely do any research as classes, homework, and course projects take up the brunt of their time. Still, I dutifully attended the weekly meetings and listened carefully to what he taught.

Not long after receiving the DURA award, our MAE department chair sent an email to all the professors and staff in the department, congratulating me and my controls professor for being accepted to conduct research at the AFRL. He sang our praises and notified the department that I was a recipient of the DURA award, would graduate that spring, and begin my Ph.D. in aerospace engineering the following semester.

Almost immediately, I received a terse email from my conceptual design professor along the lines of "I take it you will be working with the other professor for your Ph.D.?" I read that email and was certain I could hear my heart thudding in my chest. I didn't realize he had expected me to work with him for my Ph.D. In fact, I hadn't even confirmed to anyone which professor I would work with. I was simply caught up in attending classes, doing homework, focusing on my senior capstone project, and attending weekly research meetings with both professors, where I had little to nothing to update on.

I didn't respond to the email. Instead, I immediately took what felt like the longest walk from my senior design laboratory to his office as I mulled over how best to clear the air.

"Good afternoon, sir," I managed to get out.

"Good afternoon," he snapped.

Nothing seemed good about the afternoon at this point.

"Sir, I had no idea who I was going to work with for my Ph.D. I've been doing research with both of you. I got the opportunity to go to the AFRL with him and chose to go regardless of whom I end up doing my Ph.D. with.'

"Well, you can always tell when a student isn't doing good work for you and she's doing it for someone else," he retorted.

This stung and it was untrue. I hadn't been slacking off on his research and working hard on the controls research. I had been slacking off on both. How many ways can I say it, undergraduate student researchers cannot and will not deliver like graduate student researchers. They juggle too many balls, and the research ball typically gets dropped. However, there was nothing I could say to convince him otherwise. I left his office deep in thought as I tried to understand why he was so upset with me.

Five students in the senior design class had signed up to do research with him and potentially be his graduate students after finishing our undergraduate degrees. One of them decided not to go to graduate school. Another chose to go to graduate school at another university. Another's allegiance was always clear: He had always planned to work with another professor at our university for his Ph.D. The fourth student also chose another professor, but she chose him earlier in the semester. And then there was me, prevaricating till the last minute. Incapable of simply quitting his research, I chose to coast along till the decision was made for me instead of thanking him for the opportunity to learn about his work, quitting gracefully, and turning in the little I had done. I was disappointed in myself at how it played out, but I didn't realize that it would get even worse.

At the end of the semester, we all presented our senior design projects in a huge engineering classroom. The audience was large and diverse; even my department chair was present. My project team contained four of the students that did research with our professor but made other plans upon graduating. Thus, not only did he grill us more than other teams during the presentation, but I also bore the heavy brunt of his questioning. I was the controls lead on the project and he focused his questions primarily on the controls piece of the vehicle we had designed. At some point, he asked a question I couldn't answer and followed up with,

"You are the controls lead, you're about to graduate, and you don't know that?"

The vitriol was palpable, and I wished I could simply disappear, but I couldn't. I stood there and bore the retribution for my prevarication.

After my dismal presentation and Q&A, an audience member, professor, and mentor privately congratulated me and the team for a job well done.

I replied, "Thank you ma'am, but that was horrible. Our professor does not like me."

"Everyone could tell," she responded.

That was a learning experience for me. Your work and reputation will speak for you, and one incident will neither define you nor shatter that reputation. In addition, although contentious public displays with an audience can be nerve-wracking, they also give people an opportunity to see both sides and judge for themselves.

~~~~~~~~~~~~~~~~~~~~~~~~~~~~~~~

LEARN TO FLY NUGGET: THINGS HAPPEN. THERE WILL BE PEOPLE AGAINST YOU. THERE WILL BE PEOPLE FOR YOU. ACKNOWLEDGE YOUR OWN CULPABILITY BUT STAY POSITIVE BY FOCUSING ON THE PEOPLE THAT ARE FOR YOU IN TIMES OF ADVERSITY.

~~~~~~~~~~~~~~~~~~~~~~~~~~~~~~~

Of the hardworking students in the class, only one got a B: me. I wasn't surprised but I was still upset as my B felt punitive and personal.

I understand my own culpability in the incident. It's simple. I should have quit sooner. I can't help but think of the quote, "Leave when the applause is loudest." I don't know that he would have held it against me if I was the first to quit his research, but being quitter number 5 came with contempt. At the minimum, I should have made my uncommitted stance known to him. So, here's another tip: Bring your head out of the bubble of *just doing.* Try not to just go through the motions. If possible, quantify the impact of your action or inaction on the people you work or learn with. *What defines their wins? Is my win their win? Is my win their loss?*

What around them is changing and potentially affecting their wins? Know and understand the stakeholders in your life and manage them accordingly.

~~~~~~~~~~~~~~~~~~~~~~~~~~~~~~~~

LEARN TO FLY NUGGET: PAUSE AND BE PRESENT. UNDERSTAND THE RAMIFICATIONS OF YOUR ACTIONS OR INACTION. GET YOUR HEAD OUT OF THE BUBBLE OF JUST DOING OR JUST GOING THROUGH THE MOTIONS. UNDERSTAND THE DYNAMICS OF WHAT DRIVES YOUR PEERS AND SUPERIORS. LET THAT ALSO GUIDE YOUR COMMUNICATION AND HOW YOU PRESENT YOURSELF.

~~~~~~~~~~~~~~~~~~~~~~~~~~~~~~~~

Preparing to Soar

Speaking of stakeholders, remember I said to ask the professor of your favorite class if you can do research with her? In addition to the class, your affinity for the professor is also critical, especially if you are contemplating graduate school and want that professor to advise your graduate research. Your graduate success depends not on your GPA but chiefly on the number and quality of your research products, technical publications, awards, and fellowships. No one will ask if you got an A in a hypersonics class if your research reduces the loud sonic boom that prevents us from flying across the continental U.S. in one hour[31].

Your research and mental health are influenced by your thesis or dissertation advisor, who defines and guides your work. This advisor must be a mentor who can guide your research, an advocate who will speak for you behind closed doors, and a friend who wants the best for you. If you don't like that person, or vice versa, or if you both define success differently, then you may struggle. For instance, success for your professor may mean that you publish nine articles in the most highly respected journals in your field. This goal could take seven years, and if your timeline for a Ph.D. is four years and neither of you is willing to compromise, then you will butt heads.

---

[31] There is a loud noise called a sonic boom associated with a plane flying faster than the speed of sound, also called supersonic flight. Commercial supersonic flight, which drastically shortens flight time, was banned over the continental U.S. in 1973 because of the sonic boom. For context, the supersonic Concorde plane flew from New York to London in under three hours.

For a master's degree, it is not as crucial that you find the perfect professor because it has a much shorter timeline than a Ph.D. So, if your professor is the worst or if you are the worst (remember to acknowledge culpability), then at least you will both be rid of each other in two and a half years, at the longest. However, if you're doing a Ph.D., which is more of a five-year marathon than a two-year master's sprint, you must be more thorough with your decision.

I have heard a few horror stories of students' experiences with their research advisors. A company representative once visited a professor to discuss a funded research project that the professor and his graduate students would work on. The professor took him on a tour of his laboratory, where his graduate students were. "These are my slaves," he declared with a sweeping motion towards the students. Perhaps he was trying to be funny with no malicious intent. However, at least one student was hurt, and they shared that story with others. So, if research interests you, choose a class you like well enough and a professor you respect and like. Trust your gut.

I lucked out as I respected and liked my controls professor, who became my Ph.D. research advisor. We got along well and even laughed at each other's jokes. One time in class before a midterm exam, he asked if we had any questions. The class was silent until I shot up my right hand.

"I have a question, sir."

He nodded at me to go on.

"Um, how many questions will be on the exam?"

He replied, "I don't know, and it doesn't matter. You can have eight easy questions or three difficult ones. Don't focus on the number of questions but on understanding the course content."

Looking at the rest of the class, he continued with a smile,

"Does anyone have any other important technical questions like Wendy?"

I burst out laughing, and so did the rest of the class.

~~~~~~~~~~~~~~~~~~~~~~~~~~~~~~~~

LEARN TO FLY NUGGET: TRUST YOUR GUT WHEN CHOOSING A PROFESSOR WITH WHOM TO DO RESEARCH. ENSURE THAT YOU LIKE THE CLASS HE TEACHES AND THAT YOU LIKE HIM TOO.

~~~~~~~~~~~~~~~~~~~~~~~~~~~~~~~~

I liked my controls professor and looked forward to working with him closely after I completed my baccalaureate. Even after the challenges of my senior year, I still rounded out the year with honors as one of the top three graduating students in my department. I was invited to carry a banner during the graduation procession for the college of engineering, preceded only by the academic staff of deans, department chairs, and professors. This was a true honor.

An even bigger honor was my selection to give the speech at the Graduation Celebration for the entire class of 2010 alongside a Pulitzer Prize winning novelist. I spoke to the audience of almost 2000 that included my family, the entire graduating class of 2010, our university community of students, faculty and staff, and the city of Arlington, including the mayor and others.

I vividly recall telling my peers, "Some of us have jobs and know exactly what we want to do after college. Some of us, like me, don't know and so we go to graduate school to buy more time to figure it out. One thing I do know is that we can succeed in anything if we put our minds to it and stay consistent. I know this because I'm speaking to the most diligent and determined students that I've been privileged to spend the last four years of my life with."

Figure 13: Walking the stage at graduation and hugging one of my mentors and all-round favorite, Dr. T.

Two weeks after that speech, I packed my bags out of my residence hall for the very last time, got rid of my trusted but worn black Toyota Rav4 that served me well during my undergraduate years, and boarded a flight to Dayton, Ohio, where I would spend the summer at the Air Force Research Laboratory at Wright-Patterson Air Force Base.

I stared out the airplane window and reflected on the previous four years. I had accomplished my dream of being an engineer, and it wasn't by being alone. It had taken a supportive village of my family, friends, mentors, and professors. I was grateful but I was also nervously excited about the new, but wonderful, phase I was about to enter.

As I examined my upcoming Ph.D. journey, I wondered what other hurdles and routes to success lay ahead of me. Was I capable of performing meaningful research and making a unique contribution to the aerospace world? Would I one day be Dr. Wendy A. Okolo? During my undergraduate years, I had *learnt to fly*. I needed to build on that foundation now and determine exactly how far I could *soar*. I knew it wouldn't be easy, but I was prepared. Daddy did say, "When the going gets tough, the tough get going." *How hard could it be?*

LEARN TO FLY NUGGETS

JUST BECAUSE IT'S NOT REQUIRED DOESN'T MEAN YOU SHOULD SKIP IT. UNDERSTAND AND WEIGH THE FUTURE BENEFITS OF A SEEMINGLY UNNECESSARY HURDLE.

YOU WILL BE IN ROOMS WITH PEOPLE THAT HAVE MORE EXPERIENCE AND SEEM TO KNOW SO MUCH MORE. THAT'S ALRIGHT BECAUSE EVERYTHING IS FOR EVERYONE. ALWAYS GO BACK ALWAYS TO WHAT YOU KNOW. DUE DILIGENCE WILL TAKE YOU FAR.

DO RESEARCH, FOR AT LEAST ONE SEMESTER. ASK THE PROFESSOR OF YOUR FAVORITE CLASS IF YOU CAN DO RESEARCH WITH HER. UNDERGRADUATE RESEARCH EXPERIENCE WILL MAKE YOU COMPETITIVE FOR THE BEST GRADUATE PROGRAMS, JUST IN CASE YOU CONSIDER GOING TO GRADUATE SCHOOL IN THE FUTURE.

THINGS HAPPEN. THERE WILL BE PEOPLE AGAINST YOU. THERE WILL BE PEOPLE

FOR YOU. ACKNOWLEDGE YOUR OWN
CULPABILITY BUT STAY POSITIVE BY
FOCUSING ON THE PEOPLE THAT ARE
FOR YOU IN TIMES OF ADVERSITY.

PAUSE AND BE PRESENT. UNDERSTAND
THE RAMIFICATIONS OF YOUR ACTIONS
OR INACTION. GET YOUR HEAD OUT OF
THE BUBBLE OF JUST DOING OR JUST
GOING THROUGH THE MOTIONS.
UNDERSTAND THE DYNAMICS OF WHAT
DRIVES YOUR PEERS AND SUPERIORS. LET
THAT ALSO GUIDE YOUR
COMMUNICATION AND HOW YOU
PRESENT YOURSELF.

TRUST YOUR GUT WHEN CHOOSING A
PROFESSOR WITH WHOM TO DO
RESEARCH. ENSURE THAT YOU LIKE THE
CLASS HE TEACHES AND THAT YOU LIKE
HIM TOO.

BONUS LEARN TO FLY NUGGET: WHEN
THE GOING GETS TOUGH, THE TOUGH
GET GOING. GET THAT TOUGH OUT!

Epilogue

Qualified

Hold on! I have been in this Ph.D. program for almost a year, and I'm still not a Ph.D. candidate? I'm only a Ph.D. student? What's the difference and why is there one? You mean I can still be kicked out?

I slumped into my chair and stared blankly at my computer screen in my research laboratory. I momentarily considered calling my family to ask them to keep my graduate studies a secret. In fact, until I finish my Ph.D., they perhaps shouldn't tell anyone, just in case I fail out. *My God!*

I had just learned about the dreaded Ph.D. qualifying exams, simply abbreviated "Quals." However, Quals was anything from simple, and the name was a misnomer. When you are admitted to a Ph.D. program, your admission is conditional. Under the status of a Ph.D. student, you can begin course work and even research. However, after acceptance into the program, you must pass exams to indicate that you are academically competent, capable of conducting research, and will make an original research contribution to your field.

These qualifying exams are taken one to two years *after* you begin your Ph.D. program. If you pass, your status will change from Ph.D. student to Ph.D. candidate, indicating that you are now a candidate to obtain a Doctor of Philosophy degree. The hitch is that most universities in the United States, only give you two chances to pass these qualifying exams. If you fail twice, you must return to your research laboratory or office, pack your belongings, and exit the program.

Our Quals in my Mechanical and Aerospace Engineering program were mostly made up of our undergraduate course work. To be allowed to pursue a Ph.D. in one of our preferred aerospace areas, we had to demonstrate an undergraduate-level understanding of the discipline. We also had to show proficiency in a secondary aerospace discipline. *Why is one field insufficient for goodness' sake?*

This was a difficult task because I was now enrolled in graduate-level aerospace engineering classes while preparing to return to the Air Force Research Laboratory to conduct my dissertation research. I was also employed as a teaching assistant, which covered all my tuition and fees and provided a small stipend. In addition, I was in the process of applying for grants and fellowships worth more than $100,000 so I could leave my teaching assistant job and focus solely on research.

I bit my nails as I continued to glare at the airplane simulation on my computer screen. *How was I going to manage all of this while studying for the frightful Quals? I needed to ace it. I only had two chances!"*

Appendix

Learn To Fly Nuggets Compiled

- No one is exempt from adversity. Not a six-year-old child and definitely not you. That's ok. Life goes on.

- It's never too early to build your resume. Consider all you do in and outside school. Perhaps you tutor middle schoolers as a high schooler. Have a resume you can build on.

- Develop relationships with your high school teachers and community leaders that will enable you to ask for recommendation letters when you need them. Secure those letters before you leave high school if you're moving away.

- Just because it's not required doesn't mean it's not useful.

- Some people know and plan out every single goal/decision. Others don't. That's okay. Whatever you do, keep moving and know that the big picture without all the details is still a picture.

- If you are eligible, join an honors college in your university. It's a way for smart and hardworking students to academically thrive and really focus on learning.

- You don't need a bachelor's degree in aerospace engineering to work in the aerospace engineering industry. Computer scientists, mechanical engineers, electrical engineers, and many others are needed to make a plane fly and to land a rover on the moon.

- Lethargy isn't the worst thing in the world. If you're doing something well enough and consistently enough, you'll find your own path.

- "When the going gets tough, the tough get going" – Billy Ocean, but reiterated more times than you can imagine by my father.

- Explore and find what works for you with studying. It may be extra tutoring from your department or a formal study group. Don't forget the internet. Look up the complex subject and watch tutorial videos on YouTube, MIT Opencourseware, Khanacademy, etc.

- With friendships, you can be strategic/intentional, but organic friendships are the best. Don't befriend someone just because they're brilliant. Actually, be friends with them.

- When in doubt, just start. The rest will likely fall into place.

- Start strong if you can. It's easier to keep a 4.0 than to get one from a lower GPA.

- Understand how homework problems, tests, and exams are graded. Do each homework problem and submit all homework assigned.

- You can find potential mentors in student organizations. It's one sure way to meet upper classmen that can mentor you and provide guidance.

- Join and serve on the board of at least one student organization. If there isn't a chapter for a student organization you want in your school, start one and become the founder/founding member. This is a powerful boost to your resume.

- An internship is critical to securing a good job after graduating with a stem degree. Do one! If you have the time, consider a co-op too.

- Send thank you emails, expeditiously, for the small things and for the big things. To the ones you want to impress and to the ones behind the scenes. Say thank you!

- Don't get comfortable in your STEM classes if you're at a community college. Google and use the syllabi of the corresponding university courses to guide your studying so that you can be on-par with your peers when you transition to university.

- Sit close to the front, learn to listen, be kind and respectful. Your professors can see everything. Even if you are taking classes online, put your phone away and listen.

- If you're unsure about your class schedule or considering taking classes at another school, first seek the opinion of your advisor and a senior student.

- Optimize your time and be productive in between classes. This gives you more time for rest, relaxation, and enjoyment.

- Undergraduate student resumes should typically be one page long. Have 20-25 hard copies of your resume just in case electronic copies are not accepted or you are unable to print onsite at a conference.

- It's not always expensive to attend a networking conference and the costs you incur can sometimes be covered internally by the university or externally by an organization. Please ask (mentors, professors, advisors, and company representatives) and ask politely!

- Do hard things. Persisting through non-scholastic rigors teaches you discipline that will help you persevere through academic challenges.

- Give a firm handshake and look people in the eye when you are introduced. Note any identifying characteristics with the names after you meet them so you can remember their names. Use their names in conversation with them. Be present.

- Take notes during meetings to keep yourself alert. If possible, eat lunch outside and/or take quick walks outside in the fresh air to break up your day. Caffeine also helps. If you fall asleep during a meeting, give yourself some grace. It's ok.

- Learn from fellow interns. Ask what they are working on and listen actively. This will help you determine what sounds interesting and what doesn't excite you. Knowing this is helpful for a future internship, full-time position, or even targeted learning/classes back in school.

- If you don't want to ask in class, write down key concepts/reminders and any questions at the top of your notebook page and ask students or professors to explain after the class.

- If your required textbook isn't helping, (1) check your syllabus for recommended textbooks, or (2) ask your professor for recommended textbooks. You can get older editions from your library or other university libraries through a friend or interlibrary loan.

- Learn how to write simple programs if you are in an engineering field. There are free classes on YouTube, MIT Opencourseware, course era, Udacity, Stanford, and other universities. Just do a google search for free programming classes.

- In all things, give thanks. Say thank you for the little things and the big things. Be kind and polite to the janitor and to the university president. Grace and good manners will take you far.

- On your resume, quantify your contributions and achievements in scholastic and extracurricular activities. Think carefully about process improvements you have made and give yourself the credit you deserve.

- You're never really alone and can always ask for help. There are experienced people all around who either get paid to help you or are happy to help you based on their own experiences and wisdom. Seek help whenever you are stuck, confused, or overwhelmed.

- Don't forget the less popular booths at career fairs such as universities and small companies. University recruiters will share funding available to new students so you can go to school for free or at a reduced cost. Smaller companies may also be more willing to offer you an internship or job offer if the big ones don't.

- Just because it's not required doesn't mean you should skip it. Understand and weigh the future benefits of a seemingly unnecessary hurdle.

- You will be in rooms with people that have more experience and seem to know so much more. That's alright because everything is for everyone. Always go back always to what you know. Due diligence will take you far.

- Do research, for at least one semester. Ask the professor of your favorite class if you can do research with her. Undergraduate research experience will make you competitive for the best graduate programs, just in case you consider going to graduate school in the future.

- Things happen. There will be people against you. There will be people for you. Acknowledge your own culpability but stay positive by focusing on the people that are for you in times of adversity.

- Pause and be present. Understand the ramifications of your actions or inaction. Get your head out of the bubble of just doing or just going through the motions. Understand the dynamics of what drives your peers and superiors. Let that also guide your communication and how you present yourself.

- Trust your gut when choosing a professor with whom to do research. Ensure that you like the class he teaches and that you like him too.

- Remember, when the going gets tough, the tough get going. Get that tough out!

From Me to You

If you got this far and still don't have it all figured out, that's alright. Just like Astronaut Sally Ride said, "All adventures, especially into new territory, are scary." Please read on for my remarks at my university's graduation celebration on May 7th, 2010. I didn't have it all figured out then, and quite frankly, I still don't.

Thank you for such a warm introduction. I feel very blessed to be here before you today, representing the College of Engineering and the graduating class of 2010 at this year's Graduation Celebration.

Five years ago, I arrived in the United States from Nigeria. I was sixteen, and in eight days, I will graduate with honors with a bachelor's in aerospace engineering. I have come a long way and will tell you about it.

My interest in engineering as far back as elementary school when I loved solving math problems and studying the sciences. I still remember my third-grade teacher laughing at me when I told her what I wanted to be. She scoffed, "You want to be an engineer? You want to fix ceiling fans and cars? You're a girl!" Sadly, I went home and told my mother I didn't want to be an engineer anymore. I said, "I don't want to fix ceiling fans and be a mechanic!" Trust my mother to raise hell, but she was able to reaffirm my interest in engineering by telling me all the cool things that engineers did.

In four years out of high school, I have grown in many ways, formed bonds, and built relationships that I hope will last a lifetime. We all know that college is one of the most important and fulfilling times of our lives. For me, it has been a re-discovery of my myself. I am no longer the starry-eyed freshman that set foot on this campus four years ago; I have learned so much through my college career. From learning about relationships to understanding the mechanics of aircraft flying in formation, we can say that UTA has provided me with a diverse offering of knowledge.

The past four years have seen immense growth at the university. The creation of the Maverick Activities Center, the 50th anniversary of the College of Engineering along with the new engineering buildings, the creation of the SMART hospital, and so on. From having the largest freshman class in 2009 to making the first few steps towards achieving Tier One status. We may not be here when that happens, but we can rest assured that our degrees from this university will appreciate over time and a lot more once Tier One is reached.

UTA has provided me with more than just a college education. By enrolling in a school as diverse as this, we can say that I have learned a few things about other races, cultures, and nationalities. I have also learned a few phrases in Hindi, French, and Arabic while studying with my classmates.

I need to remember our family and friends and thank them for the emotional and, of course, financial support that they have provided over the past years. I know I wouldn't have been able to go through four years of aerospace engineering coursework without the pillar of support I had in the form of my family. I would also like to thank UTA and especially the Mechanical and Aerospace Engineering department, for recognizing and rewarding my every achievement; spurring me to do more and work harder.

The famous Sally Ride, the first American female astronaut who visited the university last semester, said, and I quote, "I didn't really decide that I wanted to be an astronaut for sure until the end of college." So, like some of us, she went through most of her college years without deciding on the career path she would take. Some of us have even completely gone through college without knowing exactly what we want to do, even though we will graduate with specific degrees. So, we go to graduate school to figure it out; some of us, like me.

My fellow graduates, we are at an important stage in our lives. Some might say we are at a crossroads, in which our futures are shaped by the decisions we make at this very moment. We have taken the first steps by getting an undergraduate degree, which will put us ahead. Once again, I will quote Sally Ride, who said, "All adventures, especially into new territory, are scary." Know that you are not the only student filled with a little fear as to what the future holds. Trust me, I feel it too. But just as I am sure I will be fine, I know you all will too. How do I know? Because I know who I am speaking to. I am talking to Mavericks, who are some of the greatest students and leaders I have known and spent the last four years of my life with. So, I know that you can do, to the utmost of your abilities, whatever you choose to do.

I wish you the very best in life; let's go graduate, and once again, congratulations to the U.T. Arlington Class of 2010. We did it!

Thank you!

Acknowledgments

"In everything give thanks." 1 Thessalonians 5:18.

Melissa Powers, you made me think critically about my writing and assumptions. You went above and beyond for me. Thank you for your professionalism, expertise, and timeliness.

Donald James, for writing the Foreword, for reviewing *Learn To Fly*, and for making me share, I am truly grateful. It had to be you. **Brand'ee Milton**, thank you for your design of this book. Your support is inexhaustible, and your peaceful friendship is deeply cherished.

My book reviewers **Karen Bradford, Imharia Obiagba, Kareen Okaka, Alexandra "Allie" Jannetta, Ezi Okpalaobieri, Dr. Kolawole Ogunsina,** and **Dr. Erian Armanios**, I thank you for your support and for being on "Team Wendy." Your dedicated reviews and feedback broadened my views and widened the reach of this book.

My professors, especially **Dr. Atilla Dogan**, and the support staff in the Mechanical and Aerospace Engineering department at the University of Texas at Arlington (UTA), you equipped me with the tools to become an aerospace engineer and you lauded my every achievement. The UTA Honors College, thank you for accepting me, for the financial support, and for the springboard to success you provided during my first undergraduate years. My UTA Apartment and Residence Life family, Society of Women Engineers family, and my student organizations, you taught me responsibility and the importance of an extracurricular portfolio. UTA, you are one of the best decisions I ever made.

Phyllis and **Jennifer**, you were my first friends and will always be my big sisters. Thank you for always protecting me and giving me the freedom to shine. **Ricky**, you were the first person I ever taught anything to. I love you and I am grateful for my big sisters and little brother.

Mom, thank you for giving me my first wings and showing me that I could fly. You looked after my babies while I worked on this book. Thank you for taking care of us and feeding us like your life depended on it. I love you, Mama Florence. **Daddy**, I miss you every day. Thank you for teaching me the value of hard work and for reminding me that when the going gets tough, the tough get going.

My hubby **Uche**, thank you for spoiling, protecting, and complementing me so I can focus on being, on becoming, and on thriving. Timing is everything. My **Somto** and my **Nara**. You are my absolute loves! Thank you for choosing me and for your predictable schedules. You gave me the space to begin and complete this work during my maternity leaves. I will always love you.

Love,
Wendy

About the Author

Dr. Wendy A. Okolo is an award-winning aerospace research engineer and an associate project manager at NASA Ames Research Center in Silicon Valley, California.

Her technical expertise in vehicle flight dynamics, novel control techniques, and autonomous air vehicle safety has been demonstrated by her United States patent in aerospace vehicle flight path control, numerous technical publications, research collaborations, and teaching engagements across the aerospace engineering industry, academia, and the government.

The 2021 recipient of the NASA Exceptional Technology Achievement Medal, Dr. Okolo's research experiences also include stints at the U.S. Air Force Research Laboratory (AFRL) at Wright-Patterson Air Force Base where she conducted research in aircraft formation flight for fuel savings. Her efforts were demonstrated with flight tests by the U.S. Air Force to realize easily attainable fuel efficiencies with existing and new aircraft. She also worked at the Advanced Development Programs of Lockheed Martin (Skunkworks), utilizing performance optimizing control techniques for the Joint Strike Fighter F-35C to improve efficiencies of aircraft belonging to the U.S. Naval Air Systems Command (NAVAIR). As an undergraduate aerospace student, she interned at Lockheed Martin on the Orion spacecraft, NASA's crew exploration vehicle that will facilitate human exploration beyond low earth orbit. She was also an undergraduate research assistant in flight dynamics and controls, which motivated her current research interests.

At 26 years old, Wendy became the first black woman to obtain a Ph.D. in aerospace engineering from the University of Texas at Arlington. Her graduate studies were recognized and funded by the U.S. Department of Defense through the National Defense Science and Engineering Graduate Fellowship, Zonta International through the Amelia Earhart Fellowship, the American Institute for Aeronautics and Astronautics, and the Texas Space Grant Consortium. Other research awards include a Resolution of Commendation from the Tarrant County Court of Texas and an award for excellence in research by the Women Of Color in STEM (Science, Technology, Engineering, & Mathematics). At NASA, she has received multiple awards including the 2020 NASA Ames Award for Researcher/Scientist and the

2019 NASA Ames Early Career Researcher Award. Dr. Okolo is also the recipient of the 2019 U.T. Arlington Distinguished Recent Graduate Award, the 2019 Women In Aerospace Award for Initiative, Inspiration & Impact, and the 2019 Black Engineer of the Year Award for Most Promising Engineer in U.S. Government.

Dr. Wendy A. Okolo is an avid supporter of changing the narrative of underrepresentation in STEM, particularly for young girls, career women, and people of color. She has given multiple keynotes, served on panels, and provides tools for individuals and organizations to foster diversity and inclusion in STEM.

Wendy enjoys cooking, traveling, exercising, and spending time with her husband and children. To connect with her, please visit www.wendyokolo.com